3

362.7 BUT

of related interest

How We Feel
An Insight into the Emotional World of Teenagers
Edited by Jacki Gordon and Gillian Grant
ISBN 1 85302 439 2

The Participation Rights of the Child
Rights and Responsibilities in Family and Society
Målfrid Grude Flekkøy and Natalie Hevener Kaufman
ISBN 1 85302 489 9 hb
ISBN 1 85302 490 2 pb

Child Welfare Services
Developments in Law, Policy, Practice and Research
Edited by Malcolm Hill and Jane Aldgate
ISBN 1 85302 316 7

Child Care
Monitoring Practice
Edited by Isobel Freeman and Stuart Montgomery
ISBN 1 85302 005 2

Good Practice in Child Protection
A Manual for Professionals
Edited by Hilary Owen and Jacki Pritchard
ISBN 1 85302 205 5

Child Abuse and Child Abusers
Protection and Prevention
Edited by Lorraine Waterhouse
ISBN 1 85302 408 2

Working with Children in Need
Studies in Complexity and Challenge
Edited by Eric Sainsbury
ISBN 1 85302 275 6

Children and Young People in Conflict with the Law
Edited by Stewart Asquith
ISBN 1 85302 291 8

Child Play
Its Importance for Human Development
Peter Slade
ISBN 1 85302 246 2

Understanding Drugs
A Handbook for Parents, Teachers and Other Professionals
David Emmett and Graeme Nice
ISBN 1 85302 400 7

Social Work with Children and Families
Getting into Practice

Ian Butler and Gwenda Roberts

Jessica Kingsley Publishers
London and Philadelphia

First published in the United Kingdom in 1997 by
Jessica Kingsley Publishers Ltd
116 Pentonville Road
London N1 9JB, England
and
325 Chestnut Street
Philadelphia, PA19106, USA

Second impression 1998

Library of Congress Cataloging in Publication Data
A CIP catalogue record for this book is available from the Library of Congress

British Library Cataloguing in Publication Data
A CIP catalogue record for this book is available from the British Library

ISBN 1 85302 365 5

Printed and Bound in Great Britain by
Athenaeum Press, Gateshead, Tyne and Wear

Contents

List of Figures

List of Tables

Dedication

Daniel, Elin, Ffion, Madlen, Mark, Matthew, Richard,
and to Holly Welch

Acknowledgements

Everything we know someone else taught us, although our teachers can take no responsibility for our errors and omissions; those really are all our own work. In the case of the material presented here, we acknowledge our debt to all of those colleagues with whom we worked when we were practitioners ourselves. More immediately, we acknowledge the enormous contribution made by fellow teachers on the qualifying social work course at the University of Wales, Cardiff, where most of the exercises and other teaching materials were first tried and tested. In particular, we would like to thank Dolores Davey, Penny Lloyd, Richard Hibbs, Geoff Waites and Tony Bloore. Thanks are due also to the many students who took part in our experiments. We probably learned more from them than from anyone else, except perhaps those children and families for whom we did our best (and worst) when we were social workers. Our own children and families are probably used to being left 'till last. We are very grateful for your patience and support and promise not to do this sort of thing again (until the next time). A special thanks to Pat Smail for proofreading the manuscript and the typescript and the printer's proofs.

Ian Butler and Gwenda Roberts
Cardiff
November 1996

Introduction

Any teacher will tell you that it is often the simplest questions that require the most complicated answers. What kind of work do social workers and other professionals undertake with children and families? Where does such work take place? What do you need to know in order to begin work with young people and their carers? Even the terms of the questions defy an easy definition. What exactly do you mean by 'children'? What precisely is a 'family'? This book is offered in response to such deceptively simple enquiries.

It has its origins in a series of seminars for first- and second-year students following a basic social work qualifying course. The seminars were intended to introduce participants to the nature and range of child and family social work, to provide them with opportunities to apply their broader appreciation and knowledge of social work theory and practice to work in this area and to encourage them to reflect on what they brought to the helping process. The first part of this book is intended to fulfil the same ambitions. It is aimed at those who have recently begun or who are intending to work with children and families and who recognise the need to start from first principles. The second part of the book is more directly aimed at supporting the development of specialist knowledge and skills or rather the application of generic skills in particular settings.

Of course, if we really could fully answer the questions that we began with, then this book would probably be a great deal longer than it is. It would also be the only one of its kind on the shelves. The fact that it is neither is proof enough that we do not make any exaggerated claims for it. What we aim to do in this book is to ask what are, in fact, fiendishly complex questions in such a way that the reader can provide the answers for him or herself using all the means at their disposal, including their own experience and knowledge drawn from elsewhere. The structure of the book reflects this aim in that each Unit is predicated on the active involvement of the reader, who will ideally have the opportunity to compare their developing understanding with others in the same position. Although it is perfectly possible to use this book as a self-contained introduction to child and family social work, in neither situation could it be considered a passive read. In this way it is different to other text books in this area.

It is different also in that it contains sufficient 'hard knowledge' to enable serious engagement with the key themes of social work practice with children and families but without pretensions to exhaustiveness. As such, we hope we have provided a framework through which knowledge derived elsewhere, possibly as part of a broader based social work or specific child care training, can be extended and applied.

We firmly believe that whatever interventive technologies or fashions that presently exist, or are likely to emerge in future years, ultimately it is only people who change people. In the classroom, and in this book, our aim has been to encourage social workers to better know themselves, their prejudices, strengths and limitations and what they bring to the helping process. Practitioners must be able to reflect on what they do and be able to articulate and defend their motivations, theoretical perspectives and beliefs. We hope that the process of study, reflection and application – the pattern for each Unit in this book – will impress itself upon the reader, who will then be able to 'get into practice' with children and families in both senses of the term.

How to Use this Book

The material in each Unit is arranged under headings as follows:

Course Text stands in lieu of the trainer or teacher. The course text outlines the issues under consideration and links the various themes that run through the Unit.

At the core of each Unit are a number of **Exercises** for you to complete. In the second part of the book most of the exercises are based on an extended case study.

The **Study Texts** are intended to provide you with sufficient material to complete the exercise and extend your specialist knowledge of the field.

The **Points to Consider** are prompts to consider particular issues that should arise as part of the exercise. They are also to encourage you to reflect more widely upon your answers.

The **Notes and Self-Assessment** which come at the end of each Unit provide you with an opportunity to reflect more broadly on the whole Unit.

The **Recommended Reading** is a list of three texts that we suggest you read in order to develop your understanding of the material presented in the Unit.

The **Trainer's Notes** are suggestions of how to adapt the exercise material contained in the Unit for use as the basis for working in groups.

PART I
Developing Basic Knowledge and Skills

UNIT 1
Children and Childhood

OBJECTIVES

In this unit you will:

- Reflect on your own and others' experience of childhood.
- Examine how childhood is socially constructed.
- Review the needs and rights of children.
- Explore the principle of welfare paramouncy.

PLAYING CHILDREN

As these words are being written, there is a game of cricket in progress outside. The batsman is aged six and the bowler thirteen. The six-year-old is taking the game very seriously. In between balls, he is practising shots, examining the pitch and checking for any changes to the field settings. The thirteen-year-old is messing about, running up to bowl on 'wobbly legs' and broadcasting a much exaggerated, and very loud, commentary on the game. From his desk, their father is watching the game. He is caught between the knowledge that he has to finish this chapter and desperately wanting to go out and play. By staring out of the window, he manages to do neither and, out of frustration, shouts at the players to take their game elsewhere. Which one of these three could best be described as being a child or as behaving like one?

It seems entirely appropriate that we should begin this book with a question about children. We suspect that everyone would claim to already know something about the subject and it is a sound educational principle to ask questions only when one has a reasonable expectation of receiving an answer. Its obvious who the children are, isn't it? Possibly, but on what basis do we decide? Age doesn't seem to be the determining factor. The six-year-old is the one behaving most sensibly. Physical ability doesn't seem to be decisive in that each one of them can do some things to the envy of the others. The possession of particular skills and knowledge does not seem to be helping either the thirteen-year-old or the forty-year-old. Nor do the activities in which they are engaged seem to be the deciding factors. Children and adults both write and play cricket. If we were to ask these three characters themselves how they might respond to being likened to children, the thirteen-year-old, despite his behaviour, is the one most likely to object and the forty-year-old, within reason, is the one most likely to be pleased at being mistaken for someone younger. The six-year-old wouldn't expect to be referred to as anything else. Perhaps the answer to our question is not quite so obvious after all.

Few of the everyday terms and 'common-sense' ideas encountered in social work with children and families, such as 'childhood', 'family' or 'parenthood', are as straightforward as they first appear. It is central to the purpose of this book to explore the meaning of such terms and to recognise how our understanding of them might affect our practice. If we were to look at childhood beyond this trivial example, across generations and geographical boundaries, then our sense of what the term means becomes much less obvious. What are the similarities and differences between these three lives and those of the thousands of young people who, in the thirteenth century, went off to fight in the Children's Crusade? Or with the daily lives of those children press-ganged into the eighteenth-century navy or who, not much more than a century ago, pulled wagons of coal to the surface just a few miles from where these words were written? What links the experiences of these children with the 40,000 others who will die today and every day from malnutrition or the 150 million more who live on in poor health across the world?

This Unit is about children, or, more accurately, social work in relation to our understanding of children. The first Exercise in this Unit and the Study Text which follows it are intended to widen your appreciation of the variability of childhood and encourage you to question some of the assumptions you and others may make about it.

Exercise 1.1: Images of Childhood

Assemble a selection of recent newspapers and general interest magazines. Look through them for pictures of children. All kinds of images (not just news photographs) should be included. Once you have collected about twenty images, spread them out so that you can see all of them at once.

TASKS:

1. Quickthink[1] a few words that you associate with each image.
2. Write down for what purpose you think each image is being used.
3. Write down what each image reminds you of about your own childhood or those of children for whom you are responsible.

Then complete the following sentence with at least ten different answers:

Childhood is...

Points to Consider

1. Does your collection of images suggest that childhood is experienced or represented differently depending on gender or race, for example? If so, how?
2. Would you say that there are there any universal components to the experience of childhood? If so, what are they?

---

1   Quickthinking is a little like word association. All you have to do is write down, without 'editing', as many words as you can think of that you associate with the particular stimulus or prompt.

3. Overall, do the images suggest that children are highly valued in contemporary society? What qualities/ attributes seem particularly valued?

4. Do you detect any differences between how you, as an adult, and the children in the images might describe what the image contains?

5. How much of what you understand by childhood is determined by your own experience of it?

6. Would you like to be a child again? What is attractive/ unattractive about the idea?

Study Text 1.1: The Myths of Childhood

Although Phillipe Aries' book *Centuries of Childhood* (1960) was not the first substantial critique of childhood, its influence on later thinking is difficult to exaggerate. Aries' central thesis was that in medieval society, childhood as a recognisable set of social roles and expectations did not exist and that the transition from the physical dependency of infancy to the social maturity of adulthood was unbroken. Young people quite literally occupied the same social, economic and psychological space as older people, playing, working and sharing relationships on much the same terms. According to Aries, childhood, as a distinct set of social roles and expectations, was 'discovered' in the fifteenth century, slowly diffusing throughout European society over the next three hundred years or so.

Later scholarship has called into question much of Aries' original thesis (see Archard 1993) but its enduring importance lies in the contribution it made to the development of what has been called the 'theoretically plausible space called the social construction of childhood' (James and Prout 1991, p.27). Put simply, this idea, which stems from a tradition in sociology that is concerned with the meaning rather than the function of social events and processes, implies that very little of what we associate with children or the kind of childhood that they experience is universal, fixed or certain. Rather, childhood is built up, or 'constructed', in society and is occupied by young people in much the same way that adults occupy the various social roles available to them, for example 'parent', 'worker', 'middle-aged'. Hence the meaning, social significance and experience of childhood will vary across time, even within generations and between cultures, as the society in which it is embedded changes and develops. An appreciation of childhood as a social artefact like many others and allows sociologists to ask interesting questions about why it should take a particular form at any given time and what social processes shape the social realities that young people have to face. It also allows questions to be asked about whose interests are best served by any particular construction of childhood. More importantly, understanding childhood as a social construction requires us, as adult professionals or simply as professional adults, to recognise that our account of children and childhood is not the only one possible and that our understanding of childhood may say more about us and the society we live in than it does about the real lives of the children we encounter.

Whilst it may not be the case that adults wholly determine the social facts of childhood, it is adults who write about them. Indeed, much has been written in recent years about the way in which adults invest childhood with all kinds of meanings according to their purpose at the time (see Butler 1996a). It has been argued (Butler and Williamson 1994) that the history of childhood is the history of adult myth-making about childhood and that in popular as well as social scientific terms, childhood is what adults say it is. For example, there is a strong tradition of presenting childhood as a kind of idealised age of innocence, almost as a state of grace. The French author Antoine de Saint-Exupéry's *The Little Prince* exemplifies this tradition. The story tells of how a pilot makes a forced landing in the desert. Here he meets the Little Prince who tells him stories of the planet where he lives and of his various adventures and companions and, in so doing, points the difference between the world of possibilities and the world of sordid realities and, indirectly, between the worlds of adulthood experience and childhood innocence. The Little Prince points out how adults and children see and experience quite different worlds to one another even in respect of the most mundane and commonplace objects. When the Little Prince (or any child) sees a house, for example, he or she might notice the rosy colour of the brick, the flowers in the window and the birds in the roof. The adult, looking at the same house sees only its market value.

The story of the Little Prince is a story about childhood written for adults. It is a useful reminder that children see the world differently to adults but you must judge for yourself whether, on this basis, you consider that adults are always reliable witnesses to the experience of childhood.

A sharply contrasting account to Saint-Exupéry's vision can be found in the writings of the child liberationists and radical feminists of the early seventies. John Holt's child liberationist 'manifesto' *Escape from Childhood – The Needs and Rights of Children* describes the state of childhood as 'being wholly subservient and dependent...being seen by others as a mixture of expensive nuisance, slave and super-pet' (1975, p.15). In Holt's view, even parental love is fuelled by less than disinterested motives. Children are, to their parents, no more than 'love objects' – in the same way that women have been treated by men as sex objects.

The association of the emancipatory progress of women and other subordinated groups with the experience of childhood has produced some striking rhetoric around the nature of contemporary childhood. The feminist writer Shulamith Firestone saw in the 'myth of childhood' a way for adults to compensate for all the things that are missing in their lives:

> ...it is every parent's duty to give his child a childhood to remember (swing sets, inflated swimming pools, toys and games, camping trips, birthday parties, etc.). This is the Golden Age that the child will remember when he grows up to become a robot like his father... Young adults dream of having their own children in a desperate attempt to fill up the void produced by the artificial cutoff from the young... (1979, p.40)

Consequently according to Firestone children are:

> ...burdened with a wish fantasy in direct proportion to the restraints of their narrow lives; with an unpleasant sense of their own physical inadequacy and ridiculousness; with constant shame about their dependence, economic and otherwise ('Mother, may I?'); and humiliation concerning their natural ignorance of practical affairs. Children are repressed at every waking minute. Childhood is hell. (1979, p.50)

Despite their obvious differences, what both of these romantic and radical accounts of childhood have in common is the recognition, after Aries, that contemporary childhood is clearly separated from adulthood psychologically, emotionally, economically and culturally. Both accounts also attest to the relative powerlessness of children to be significant authors of their own biographies, both literally and figuratively.

Many social work constructions of childhood reflect particular views of this 'otherness' of children. For example, many social workers – particularly those steeped in the developmental psychologies of Freud, Jung and Adler – understand childhood almost exclusively as a state of becoming, not one of being. The primary value of childhood in such accounts lies in its simultaneous use as a preparation for adulthood and its capacity to ensure the stability of social and cultural norms. Childhood is understood merely as a transitional process driven by a fury of evolutionary, biological and hormonal imperatives until the advent of the staid, middle-aged individual of modest, moderate and settled needs. Some accounts of childhood accentuate the influence of other children in the socialisation process and focus on the peer group as a factor in the production and maintenance of (usually deviant) behaviour. Other accounts reflect the relative powerlessness of children to prevent their victimisation by adults.

A common thread running through many such accounts of the 'otherness' of childhood is the way in which the experience of children is presented and largely understood in terms of their incapacities and *naïveté* rather than in terms of their strengths and experiences. Such deficit models of childhood can imply that childhood is less subtle, complex and meaningful than adulthood and consequently less interesting, valuable and important.

It is not our purpose to persuade you to any particular understanding or view of childhood. Our aim is to encourage you to reflect on what images of childhood you carry around with you and to question the attitudes, values and knowledge that inform your particular view. By being aware of the presumptions that you bring to your understanding of the circumstances of specific children, we hope that you will meet each individual child on his or her own terms without imposing your meanings on their lives.

NEEDS AND RIGHTS

We can see how the contested nature of childhood has a direct bearing on social work practice by exploring the apparent opposition that is sometimes established between children's needs and children's rights. At a general level, the proponents of a rights-based model for practice might argue that an emphasis on children's particular needs tends to infantalise them well beyond the period of their infancy. It might also be the case that talk of needs sometimes derives from a desire to impose adult constructions upon children's lives, such as when an adult says that a child 'needs' a 'highly structured and controlling environment' when what they mean is that they want the child to be locked up; or when a child is said to need 'clear boundaries and explicit means of discipline' when what is intended is that the child should be subjected to corporal punishment. One commentator has advised children that whenever 'they hear the word "need", [they should] reach for their solicitor' (Shaw 1989, p.2). On the other hand, an advocate of a needs-based approach might acknowledge that, whilst it is perfectly possible to use the rhetoric of rights to protect the integrity of individual children and to encourage them to play their full part in civil society, it is also the case that 'rights-speak' can look suspiciously like neglect when it leaves eight-year-olds 'free' to carry automatic weapons or to be exploited and sexually abused in brothels and backstreets.

The social work task is located right at the centre of such apparent contradictions. How you resolve them in practice will depend on the particular image or construction of childhood that you bring to your work as much as on the particular theoretical frameworks that you bring from your knowledge of the social sciences or elsewhere. The following exercise is intended to sensitise you to your understanding of children's needs and rights and to explore further the particular model of childhood to which you currently subscribe.

	Needs	*Rights*
Person aged 0–5	1. 2. 3. 4. 5.	1. 2. 3. 4. 5.
Person aged 5–10	1. 2. 3. 4. 5.	1. 2. 3. 4. 5.
Person aged 10–18	1. 2. 3. 4. 5.	1. 2. 3. 4. 5.
Person aged over 18	1. 2. 3. 4. 5.	1. 2. 3. 4. 5.

Figure 1.1 Needs/rights grid

Exercise 1.2: Needs and Rights

Using the grid (above), write down what you consider to be the most important needs and rights of the individuals concerned.

Points to Consider

1. How important is the age of the individual to any consideration of his/her needs or rights?

2. Would your account of needs or rights be different if the individuals were differentiated by race, gender or disability? If so, how?

3. Does an individual have a right to have all of his/her needs met?

4. How far does an individual have a need to be able to exercise his/her rights?

5. Compare the words that you have used to describe rights and those you have used to describe needs. What does the difference tell you about how you regard the two concepts?

6. What does your understanding of needs and rights tell you about your own construction of childhood? Where would you stand on a continuum that ran from maternalism/paternalism at one end to radical liberationist at the other?

Study Text 1.2: The Needs and Rights of Children

CHILDREN'S NEEDS

Even if we thought we could, we do not intend to provide you with a comprehensive check-list of the needs of a child, appropriate to its every age and stage of development. To do so would suggest that such needs inventories or maps are more fixed and consensual than they are. Nor would we wish to imply that social work can be done 'by numbers' or entirely on the basis of received wisdom. However, you may find it helpful to compare the list of needs that you produced for the last Exercise with the categorisations provided in Figure 1.1. You should refine and develop

Mia Kellmer Pringle (1974)

- Love and security
- New experiences
- Praise and recognition
- Responsibility

Christine Cooper (1985)

- *Basic physical care*: e.g. warmth, shelter, food, rest and protection
- *Affection*: e.g. physical contact, admiration, tenderness, patience, companionship
- *Security*: e.g. continuity of care, consistent patterns of care and daily routine, harmonious family group
- *Stimulation of innate potential*: e.g. praise, encouragement, educational stimulation
- *Guidance and control*: e.g. examples of honesty and a concern for others, discipline, to develop socially acceptable behaviour
- *Responsibility*: e.g. to practise decision-making skills and to gain experience through mistakes
- *Independence*: at first about small things but 'over-protection is as bad as too early responsibility and independence' (p.61)

Margaret Bryer (1988)

- *Physical*: e.g. medical care, possessions, shelter, space, fresh air and exercise, physical affection, adequate financial resources, discipline and control
- *Educational*: e.g. knowledge of culture, knowledge of own background, play and hobbies, holidays, sex education, formal education
- *Social*: e.g. friends, interest groups, to be a member of the community, to express individuality
- *Ethical*: e.g. aesthetic sense, sense of identity, values, self-respect, opportunity to practise religion
- *Emotional*: e.g. trust, praise, individual attention, loyalty, love, security, privacy, understanding, fun and laughter

Figure 1.2 Some models of children's needs

your understanding of children's needs and general development through further reading and by direct observation of children but, as you do so, you should also consider some general points about the maturational process and the needs of children.

First, the speed of development, particularly of very young children, is one of the real wonders of the natural world. The proverbial cry of 'My, hasn't s/he grown!' from friends or relatives who have only occasional contact with a child has a real basis in fact. If you consider that in a little over four years most of those snuffling new-born bundles of sensation and smells are transformed into neat rows of schoolchildren making their first attempts to put their 'news' down on paper, then you would probably agree that the rate of change is breathtaking. In focusing on any child's needs, at any age, be aware of the amazing pace of change and do not trap a child into a pattern of needs that s/he has long outgrown.

Second, be mindful of the complexity of all human beings. There is infinite variety in the interaction of all human needs and no-one, at any age, should be reduced to only one or two dimensions of their personalities or attributes. It is never appropriate to focus all our effort on meeting the physical needs of a child if we fail to meet its social or emotional needs, to take an obvious example. (This point is returned to in Units 7 and 8). Children, just like everyone else, have to be considered holistically and their needs understood as dynamic rather than fixed and enduring.

Third, whatever our views on the determining influence of genetic inheritance or environmental influence (nature versus nurture), we would all probably agree that each human being is unique and individual. All babies do not look the same! Nor do all five-year-olds act or think in the same way or have identical needs, any more than all forty-year-olds do.

CHILDREN'S RIGHTS

The enfranchisement of any subordinated group is always a slow and halting process and the contemporary debate on children's rights is of relatively recent origin. It wasn't until 1991 that Peter Newell was able to declare that children's rights had 'come of age' (p.xi). The legitimacy of children's claims to rights, and indirectly the occasion of Newell's remarks, was the adoption by the United Nations General Assembly in November 1989 of the Convention on the Rights of the Child. You might usefully compare the list of rights that you have devised with those established by the Convention (see Figure 1.2).

It is possible, with only a little distortion, to group those rights defined by the Convention into four categories: survival rights (e.g. Art. 6); development rights (e.g. Art. 28); protection rights (e.g. Art. 34); participation rights (e.g. Art. 13). Specific formulations of the first three groups of rights – which we might describe together as 'nurturance rights' (see Rogers and Wrightsman 1978) – might command wide acceptance (although you should note that many countries, including the United Kingdom, have entered specific reservations concerning the Convention and do not accept all of its provisions.) It is probably the case that many of the rights that you described in Exercise 1.2 were broadly of this type. In practice, such rights may represent, at worst, little more than good intentions and, at best, be no more than a reflection of current ideas of what constitutes children's needs. For the most part, rights of this type, even if they are enforceable in law (e.g. the right to education), are defined and enforced by adults on the child's behalf. The fourth group of rights, participation rights, are of a different order in that they have 'self determination orientations' (Rogers and Wrightsman 1978) and so make a case not for 'welfare' but for 'liberty' (Franklin 1995). It is rights of this sort that pose the greatest challenge to the dominant deficit models of childhood that we described in Study Text 1.1 and which provide the liveliest debates in social work with children and their families.

There are a number of arguments and counter arguments that are routinely made concerning the exercise of children's participation rights. For example:

- *Children are not sufficiently rational or intellectually capable of making competent choices.* In the case of infants this will be true but it does seem that children's capacity for rational thought is considerably greater than most adults are prepared to credit. We know of no research findings which suggest that the social world of children is less subtle, complex and nuanced than that of adults. Also, if reason and intellectual capacity rather than age are the criteria, then many adults should be denied their rights too.

- *Children lack sufficient experience on which to base their decisions, which can only develop with maturity.* This might be considered a self-fulfilling prophecy in the light of the previous argument and does seem to rest on a touching faith in the capacity of humans to learn from their mistakes. This argument usually rests on a

As well as establishing some important general principles, the Convention establishes the following rights for children:

- The inherent right to life (Article 6)

- The right to have a name from birth and to be granted nationality (Article 7)

- The right to live with parents (unless incompatible with best interests), the right to maintain contact with parents if separated (Article 9)

- The right to leave any country and to enter their own in order to be reunited with parents or to maintain the child-parent relationship (Article 10)

- The right to express an opinion and to have that opinion taken into account in matters affecting the child (Article 12)

- The right to freedom of expression (Article 13)

- The right to freedom of thought, conscience and religion (Article 14)

- The right to freedom of association (Article 15)

- The right to protection from interference with privacy, family, home and correspondence (Article 16)

- The right of access to appropriate information that promotes social, spiritual and moral well-being (Article 17)

- The right to be protected from abuse and neglect (Article 19);

- The right to special protection for those children deprived of a family environment (Article 20)

- The right to special protection for refugee children (Article 22)

- The right of children with disabilities to special care, education and training (Article 23)

- The right to the highest level of health possible and to health and medical services (Article 24)

- The right to periodic review of placement for children placed by the State for reasons of care, protection or treatment (Article 25)

- The right of children to benefit from social security including social insurance (Article 26)

- The right to an adequate standard of living (Article 27)

- The right to education (Article 28)

- The right of children of minority communities and indigenous peoples to enjoy their own culture and to practice their own religion and language (Article 30)

- The right to leisure, play and participation in cultural and artistic activities (Article 31)

- The right to be protected from the exploitation of their labour (Article 32)

- The right to be protected from drug abuse (Article 33)

- The right to be protected from sexual exploitation (Article 34)

- The right to be protected from sale, trafficking and abduction (Article 35)

- The right to respect for human and civil rights in relation to the administration of justice (Article 40)

Figure 1.3 The UN Convention on the Rights of the Child

confusion between 'the right to do something [and] doing the right thing' (Franklin 1995, p.11) and if the ill-judged consequences of the exercise of certain rights are sufficient to deny those rights then a similar argument should, logically, apply to many adults too.

- *Children are not self-sufficient and, as dependent creatures, do not qualify as full stakeholders in civil society.* On this basis almost everyone might be denied their rights to some degree but certainly those who are ill, elderly or with a disability would be denied theirs.

- *Children's rights can only be achieved at the expense of the inalienable rights of parents.* We explore the changing balance of power between parents and children in Unit 3, although this argument is usually only a thinly disguised attempt to protect the institution of the family from the inquisitorial attentions of the State. This, in turn, is sometimes only a thinly disguised argument for the dismantling of welfare provision of all sorts and contains echoes of the 'no such thing as society' point of view which makes all talk of civil rights redundant.

CONCLUSION

Underlying the debate about needs versus rights we see a glimpse of the central dynamic of childhood itself, the progress from dependency to autonomy, which, as we have indicated, is a matter of debate. In reality it is neither necessary nor helpful to think of 'needs' and 'rights' as opposites or as mutually exclusive concepts. Both 'needs-speak' and 'rights-speak' are useful correctives to one another. The biological dependency of infants, for example, calls forth a primal and beneficial concern for the nurturance and protection of children. Similarly, in a society in which children are exploited and abused it is important that children possess a civil and legal status from which they can defend their interests.

The progress from dependency to autonomy is not the only dynamic along which childhood operates. It moves also between powerlessness and the possession of power, between innocence and experience and between a state of nature and a state of grace. The precise point at which you locate the circumstances and experiences of each child whom you encounter will be a function not just of the characteristics of the child him or herself but of the image of childhood that you bring to the encounter. If you believe that children should be seen much more than heard, if you think that *Lord of the Flies* rather than *Swallows and Amazons* captures the true essence of childhood experience or if you believe that children are 'nasty, brutish and short' rather than 'wonderful and charming creatures...[with minds] all hung round with such bright vivid things' (Virginia Woolf *A Writer's Diary*) then you will, in all likelihood, find a plausible justification for your views in the conduct or circumstances of the child concerned.

It is axiomatic in social work practice generally that the attitudes and values that you bring to your work are critical to the process and outcome of any intervention. In training, social workers are required to demonstrate that they are able to 'identify and question their own values and prejudices, and their implications for practice' in order that they become 'self aware and critically reflective' practitioners (CCETSW 1995, p.18). In working with children in particular, it is just as important that you are aware of your particular construction of childhood and that you are able to explain and defend it when required. Returning to the central dynamic of dependency/autonomy, the next exercise will help you to determine your current position and how well you can articulate it.

 ### Exercise 1.3: Needs and Rights in Action

Read the text of Article 16 of the UN Convention on the Rights of the Child and think how you might apply its provisions in the situations described below. You should supply whatever additional material you need in order to determine your response.

> No child shall be subjected to arbitrary or unlawful interference with his or her privacy, family, home or correspondence, nor to unlawful attacks on his or her honour or reputation. Article 16 (Part)

1. You are the responsible social worker and a young person asks you if they can make a private phone call to their father who is accused of abusing him/her.

2. You are visiting a children's home and the young person you are seeing tells you that another young person is in possession of stolen goods.

3. Whilst on duty in your agency you overhear a conversation between two young people in which one tells the other that she thinks she is pregnant and is too scared to tell anyone else.

4. On a holiday you are planning for children known to your agency you are asked to keep an eye on one young person's contact with another as it is believed that they are planning to commit a serious crime together.

5. The headteacher of a young person for whom you are responsible asks you for a copy of previous case conference minutes 'for the records'.

6. After a series of attacks on residents your agency wants to install closed-circuit TV in a children's home. One of the cameras will unavoidably overlook the residents' recreational space.

7. You believe that a young person for whom you are responsible is injecting proscribed drugs. During a visit to the young person you have the opportunity to search their room without their permission but with no risk of being observed.

8. A colleague has written a damning court report on a family based on what you know to be inaccurate information. A member of the family concerned asks you what the report says.

9. The parent of a teenager for whom you are responsible tells you that their son/daughter is enuretic and would you 'have a word' with them.

10. A child that you are working with is described as an abuser in a local newspaper. The opposite is in fact the case. You are asked by a reporter for your comments.

Points to Consider

1. Do children need privacy?

2. Are the limits on a child's right to privacy any different to those you would tolerate for yourself?

3. What, if any, needs have priority over a child's right to privacy?

4. Is your professional obligation to maintain confidentiality helped or hindered by a child's right to privacy?

5. In whose interests are you working when/if you decide to set limits on a child's right to privacy?

6. How would you integrate Article 16 into your own practice?

THE BEST INTERESTS OF THE CHILD

However one might describe or categorise any particular construction of childhood, it seems likely that its proponents hold the views that they do out of a sincere commitment to do what is 'best for the child'. The UN Convention on the Rights of the Child is premised on such a belief:

> In all actions concerning children, whether undertaken by public or private social welfare institutions, courts of law, administrative authorities or legislative bodies, the best interests of the child shall be a primary consideration. (Article 3)

Inevitably, perhaps, the 'best interests of the child' is yet another of those terms that defies a simple or consensual definition. It too is dependent on how one understands the nature and the experience of childhood as much as it depends on a particular set of life circumstances. However, in social work terms, determining the best interests of the child cannot remain simply a matter of philosophical or sociological speculation. It is a professional imperative and, in some cases, a statutory requirement. The Children Act 1989 (the Act) provides an important account of what is meant by the best interests of the child.

The relationship between social work practice and the law (Braye and Preston-Shoot 1992) is a complex one and needs to be understood in a broader context than this book allows. A standard text book on social work and the law takes the view that:

> [social workers] were created to perform – and only to perform – the jobs that Parliament has given you. Although there is plenty of room for good intentions, these do not define your job; the statutes do. The statutes tell you who you have responsibilities towards, and how they shall be exercised. (Brayne and Martin 1990, p.1)

Whilst this implies a very narrow understanding of the social work task, it is perhaps more true now than it has been in previous years. It is unarguably the case that contemporary child care practice is significantly determined by the provisions of the Children Act 1989. The Act and associated Regulations and Guidance have achieved almost talismanic status in that their authority is routinely sought for any intervention in the life of a child. Yet the source of that authority is rarely questioned (but see Parton 1991). A brief discussion of the Children Act 1989 as a political act, like any other, is given in Study Text 3.4. At this stage, however, we require only that you regard the provisions of the Act as an important reference point and not necessarily as the final arbiter of good practice. The Act, like all of its predecessors, will one day have to be re-written.

In reading the final Study Text of this Unit, which describes the model of 'best interests' that governs decision making in the courts, you should consider what image of childhood lies beneath the text of the Act and in the decisions of courts and reflect on how closely it approximates to your own.

Study Text 1.3: The Welfare Principle

The Children Act 1989 refers not to the 'best interests of the child' but to the 'welfare of the child' which shall be the court's 'paramount consideration'[2] when it determines any question concerning the upbringing of a child or the administration of his/her property (CA 1989, s.1(1)). This is essentially a re-enactment of a principle established in English law by the Guardianship of Infants Act 1925 (and incorporated into the now repealed Guardianship of Minors Act 1971). Lord MacDermott's interpretation, made under the old law, still provides an authoritative gloss on what is usually referred to as the welfare principle, which he described as:

> a process whereby, when all the relevant facts, relationships, claims and wishes of parents, risks, choices and other circumstances are taken into account and weighed, the course to be followed will be

---

2   Note that this duty applies to courts only. It does not apply to parents or to the actions of local authorities. Unit 3 explores the duties that attach to a child's parents and Unit 5 describes the lesser duty on local authorities to 'safeguard and promote' (CA 1989, s.17) the welfare of the child.

that which is most in the interests of the child's welfare as that term is now understood. *J v C* [1969] 1 All ER 788 at 820–821[3]

The welfare of the child is to be considered 'before and above' any other consideration (Lord Chancellor, *Hansard*, HL vol.502, col.1167), even the essential justice of the case.

The Act itself contains no definition of 'welfare'. It does, however, provide a check-list of factors which courts are required to consider in particular circumstances; namely, when the court is considering making an order under Part IV of the Act (care and supervision orders) or when it is determining a contested application under s.8. The check-list *may* be used in other circumstances, of course. The items on the check-list are not presented in any particular order and none is automatically any more important than the other. As Lord Justice Dunn has observed: '...the circumstances of each individual case are so infinitely varied that it would be unwise to rely on any rule of thumb, or any formula, to try and resolve the difficult problem which arises on the facts of each individual case' (*Pountney v Morris* [1984] FLR 381 at 384D).

The check-list comprises seven items, as follows (s.1(4)):

- The ascertainable wishes and feelings of the child concerned (considered in the light of his age and understanding): the court retains its discretion as to how much weight it should attach to the wishes and feelings of the child, which will vary according to the nature of the subject matter of the application but it does have to consider them. This means that social workers and others will have first to obtain them. The question of the child's age and understanding (also discussed in Study Text 3.4) is to be understood as a developing one whereby with increasing competence comes increasing influence. The Court of Appeal has held (in *M v M (Removal from Jurisdiction)* [1993] 1 FCR 5) that the wishes and feelings of a 10- and 11-year-old, both

---

3   References to particular cases are given in the form that lawyers conventionally adopt when citing cases. The first element refers to the parties to the case, then the year and then the paragraphs or page number of the particular series of law reports where the case is described. There are several different series of law reports. For our purposes, the most frequently cited are the Family Law Report (FLR) and the All England Law Report (All ER).

intelligent and articulate, should have had considerable weight attached to them.

- His physical, emotional and educational needs: the court will expect to be informed of the day-to-day arrangements in place to secure the basic physical care of the child. Courts have shown a preference for stability in a child's daily routine (*Re B (A Minor) (interim Custody)* [1983] FLR 683). In terms of meeting a child's emotional needs, courts have shown a strong preference for keeping brothers and sisters together, for maintaining an enduring relationship with both parents and for placement with family members rather than non-relatives where that is possible. As Lord Scarman has observed (*Re (SA) (A Minor)* [1984] 1 All ER 289 at 292): 'A home with his natural parents, if circumstances are right and a loving relationship exists, must be best'. However, the 'if' is a significant one: '…of course there is a strong supposition that, other things being equal, it is in the interests of the child that it shall remain with its natural parents. But that has to give way to particular needs in particular situations' (Lord Donaldson in *Re H (A Minor) (Custody: Interim Care and Control)* [1991] 2 FLR 109). Courts may interpret educational needs broadly and may consider the arrangements made by carers to promote the child's education, including, for example, the capacity of a parent to balance the competing demands of homework and television (*May v May* [1986] 1FLR 325).

- The effect of any change: courts have shown a marked preference for the *status quo*, especially in relation to younger children, provided that the *status quo* is satisfactory. This preference is strengthened considerably by the provisions of s.1(5) of the Act, the 'non-intervention principle', which prohibits the court from making any order in a case unless it considers doing so 'would be better for the child than making no order at all.'

- The child's characteristics: subject to the overriding commitment to the paramouncy of the child's welfare, courts have shown a preference for placing younger children, particularly girls, with their mothers. It has also been held that a girl approaching puberty would be better placed with her mother and that a boy aged eight, as a general rule, would be better placed with his father. Courts have also had regard to racial and cultural factors in determining where the child's welfare will best be served.

- Harm: 'harm' in this context, and elsewhere in the Act, means 'ill-treatment or the impairment of health or development' (s. 31 (9). See Study Text 10.1). Courts are able to consider *any* harm done to the child and, in determining the likelihood of harm, may take into account the harm done by a proposed carer to any other child or adult.

- The capacity of parents and others: in the course of proceedings parties may wish to parade every piece of evidence relating to the alleged past incapacities of other parties, whereas courts will primarily be concerned with the carer's capacity to care for the child in the future. The question of capacity is not the same as intention and courts do not have to have regard to the 'best interests' of parents in determining their capacity to care for a child. The financial circumstances of carers, whilst a consideration, is not usually a determining factor.

- The powers of the court: in effect, any court may make any order under the Act – although not all orders may be made simply by the court's own motion; some may only be made on the application of an interested party. This provision ensures that the court is best able to tailor its decision to the particular circumstances of the child, although the provisions of the 'non-intervention principle' apply to all proceedings under the Act.

The Act makes one further specific provision concerning the welfare of the child and the court process, namely that delay in proceedings is likely to 'prejudice the welfare of the child' (s.1(2)). A distinction is to be made between purposeful delay where time may be taken in order to resolve a particular problem or to determine the effect of particular circumstances and damaging drift (Butler *et al.* 1993).

CONCLUSION

The history of the study of childhood is the history of adults' study of childhood and any adult construction of childhood seems to be constructed differently – both to how childhood itself was experienced or is currently being lived. The adult world, including the social work world, is littered with the never-consulted casualties of the social worker who 'knew best' or 'knew already'. Recognising the 'otherness' of childhood, expecting and respecting difference, and accepting the limits of one's own experience and understanding of the process are absolute prerequisites to working in the child's best interests.

The images of childhood that you bring to your work exert a powerful influence on the kind of social worker you are and the kind of work that you do. On the basis that you will frequently find what you are looking for, we hope that you will make a strenuous and conscious effort to meet each child that you encounter as they really are and not as you remember, imagine or would like them to be.

NOTES AND SELF ASSESSMENT

1. When does childhood begin and end? When did you stop being a child?

2. What does it mean to be treated like a child?

3. In what ways do you treat children differently to adults?

4. What potential for oppressive practice does your own construction of childhood have?

5. What do you think you have to learn from the children with whom you work?

6. How does your image of childhood help you to help children?

RECOMMENDED READING

Archard, D. (1993) *Children – Rights and Childhood*. London: Routledge.

Butler, I. and Williamson, H. (1994) *Children Speak: Children, Trauma and Social Work*. London: Longman.

Hoyles, M. (ed) (1979) *Changing Childhood*. London: Writers and Readers Publishing Co-operative.

TRAINER'S NOTES

Exercise 1.1: Images of Childhood

As well as newspapers and magazines, film and TV programmes are other sources of images – although the very best source is the family photograph album. This exercise works equally well if participants are asked to provide written accounts of childhood from their own reading, especially their childhood reading. Similarly, any book of quotations will provide a list of concise and challenging accounts of childhood. Whatever the graphic or written stimulus however, the liveliest discussion and the clearest reminiscences of childhood are produced by the purchase and consumption of the participant's favourite childhood sweets!

Exercise 1.2: Needs and Rights

This exercise can be started as a large group and some quickthinking of both needs and rights. These needs and rights can then be attributed to various categories of individuals distinguished by age, gender, race, etc, either in a large group or in smaller groups. Alternatively, a wide range of needs and rights can be written onto cards beforehand and, either as a large group or a series of smaller groups, they can be attributed to various categories. Discussion can be encouraged if there is a lack of consensus over any particular attribution.

Exercise 1.3: Needs and Rights in Action

A large group can be split into three smaller groups, one representing the child concerned, one the parent or carer of the child and the other the social worker. The several groups could then negotiate a consensus on the application of the right to privacy in each mini-scenario. This exercise works particularly well if tailored to the particular work or placement setting of group members. Participants can be encouraged to develop 'Practice Guidelines' for their particular work or practice learning context and to bring the views of colleagues back to the group for discussion.

UNIT 2

The Family

OBJECTIVES

In this unit you will:

- Consider the variety of family forms and household structures to be found in contemporary Britain.
- Explore your personal construction of the family.
- Consider the experience of family life from a gendered perspective.
- Explore critical issues in working with Black families.

 **MEET THE FAMILY**

Consider these two appreciations of the family:

> It is central to our national life. It is the basic building block of our community. It is the place where education begins, where our habits and lifestyles are formed and where our characters are moulded. I strongly believe that the family should be more than simply a group of people with keys to the same house or flat... We want to do all that we can to promote the interests of the family. We must help marriages, which may be made in heaven, but on which the maintenance work must be done by men and women.

> Family life, family values, decent normal family fun, family shopping, family leisure. The word is used these days as the word 'Aryan'

14. Are more or fewer people marrying?

15. Which is higher, the divorce rate or the marriage rate?

16. What proportion of marriages are remarriages?

17. What proportion of women below the age of 50 are cohabiting?

18. What percentage of divorces involve children?

19. How many children per week are involved in divorce?

20. Is the number of children involved in divorce rising or falling?

 **Points to Consider**

1. On what sources of knowledge/information did you base your answers to these questions?

2. What are the usual sources of information about household structure and family formation to which the general public have access?

3. Would you say that you have tended to over- or under-estimate the variations that exist in family form? Why might this be?

4. Do you regard any of the rates or proportions that you have noted as actually too high or too low? Which one(s) and why?

5. Which, if any, of the rates or proportions that you have identified do you regard as problematic? Should anything be done about the state of affairs described?

6. How far can statistics help you to decide what is a 'typical' family? What is the difference between a 'typical' family and a 'normal' one?

Study Text 2.1: Family Fortunes – The Facts of Family Life

This Study Text provides a digest of statistics drawn from government sources that bear on the social realities of household structure and family form in the UK. It is highly selective and is intended to illustrate patterns of continuity as well as change, although it does focus particularly on emerging demographic trends and phenomena.

HOUSEHOLDS[2]

In 1991 over a quarter of all households in Great Britain were one-person households, a proportion that has doubled in the thirty years from 1961. The average household size has decreased over the same period from 3.1 persons to 2.5 (CSO 1994, Table 2.2). The average size of household varies substantially by the ethnic origin of the head of the household. The mean size of households headed by someone of Bangladeshi or Pakistani origin is almost twice the overall mean at 4.76 persons, for example (NCH 1996, Table 1.4). Given that the distribution of ethnic minority communities is subject to wide regional variations, average household size will also vary from locality to locality.

Despite the growth of single-person households, the single most common type of household in Great Britain is the married couple without children (28% in England; 21% in Northern Ireland). The second most common is the married couple with either one or two children (22% in Wales and Northern Ireland; 20% in England). Lone-parent households (with children) constitute 6 per cent of households in England and Wales and 8 per cent of households in Scotland (CSO 1994, Table 2.5). Taken together, families with children outnumber families without children.

---

2   A household is defined for statistical purposes as 'a person living alone or a group of people who have the address as their only or main residence and who either share one meal a day or share the living accommodation' (Central Statistical Office (CSO) 1994, p.180)

national boundaries, ensures that any definition of the 'family' is likely to be partial, in both senses of the word. One commentator has noted that:

> ...if not only family form, family activity, family functioning but also the emotional interior of the family is highly variable, then it is questionable whether the term 'family' should be dispensed with... 'family' would appear to refer neither to a specific empirical type nor to a theoretical type... (Harris 1984, p.246)

The almost infinite range of relationships, domestic arrangements, social circumstances and personal networks to which the term has been applied means that it can be used in the service of almost any political ideology. The views expressed above by John Patten are typical of a post-war, cross-party view of the family as functional to social order, social cohesion and consensus. That is not to say that certain family forms are not preferred by some legislators. For example, a local authority is forbidden by law to: 'promote the teaching in any maintained school of the acceptability of homosexuality as a pretended family relationship' (Local Government Act 1988, s.28).

Similarly, the vilification of lone-parents by certain politicians over recent years has been a recurrent strand to a variety of 'back to basics' crusades. It is not our intention to debate the social policy response to the changing fortunes of the family (but see Van Every 1992) or to characterise particular ideological orientations to the family (but see Study Text 3.4) or even to explore the sociological analyses that inform and illumine them (but see Cheal 1991). Our point is that, just as we saw in relation to children and childhood, as well as a wide variety of social 'facts' that need to be accommodated in our understanding of the term, there are a wide range of deeply held beliefs about the family that we need to appreciate as a prelude to working effectively in this field. The next exercise will begin to sensitise you to some of the attitudes you have towards the family.

Exercise 2.2: Is this a Family?

Decide which of these households is a family and why. You may find the following criteria useful in determining family status:

- the degree of emotional commitment
- the degree of commitment to the future of the arrangements
- the degree of emotional interdependence
- the degree to which social and domestic life is interwoven
- the degree of financial interdependence
- the intimacy of the relationship(s)
- the duration of relationship(s)
- the exclusivity of relationship(s).

Note any other criteria that occur to you as you complete the exercise.

1. John and Jane are both students in their early twenties. They have shared a flat for nearly three years and divide all the household bills between them. They have bought some furniture and household items together. They eat together, spend a lot of time in each others company and frequently go out with each other socially. Over the last few months they have slept together but both have had intimate relationships with others at the same time. When they leave college, John plans to return to his home area. Jane is thinking of travelling abroad for a year or two.

2. Betty and George have been married for eight years. They hardly speak to one another except to argue or to 'sort out' practical matters to do with the children, Jo aged four and Chris aged six. Betty has a long-standing relationship with another man. Both pay their wages into separate accounts, although each pays half of the household bills. Betty does most of the necessary child care during the week and George takes over at weekends.

3. Surinder is a lone parent. She cares for her daughter, Shama, aged ten. Shama's father does not support the family financially. He is married and has three other children of his own. He regularly

as *the* family. That a family can be an oppressive, cruel and hopeless environment for some children…should be sufficient to remind us that it is a dangerous assumption to leave entirely undifferentiated the interests of children and their parents (Butler and Williamson 1994, p.9).

As well as differentiating between the interests and experiences of parents and children, it is important to differentiate the experience of family life according to gender. The following exercise, and the Study Text which follows, will clarify what we mean.

Exercise 2.3: A Day in the Life

Consider the following descriptions of a day in the life of the Gorman family, provided by Doreen and John Gorman, then compare their accounts against the criteria you developed for the purposes of Exercise 2.2. You may wish to add to that list these additional measures:

- the degree of personal autonomy that each has
- the nature and extent of social networks to which each has access
- the relative social status that each might have in the eyes of others
- the degree of control over their time and labour that each has.

The Gormans have been married for 25 years. They have four children, three of whom are still living at home. John Gorman is 47 and works at a local factory. Doreen is 41 and works part-time. They live on a large housing estate in a home they are buying through a housing association.

John: I get up every morning at six and take a cup of tea to Doreen. If she's been at work the previous night, I'll leave her to lie in till I leave for work at quarter to seven and I'll wake the two youngest for school. I don't usually bother with breakfast. I drive to work, which takes me about an hour through the traffic. I've been doing this for years but I still hate the journey. Its all stop, start, stop, start. I have to be in work by 8 a.m. I don't enjoy my job but I don't hate it either, like some of the lads at work do. It can be a laugh some times and I have got some good mates at work.

We usually get out for half-an-hour at lunchtime and have a bit of a kick-around with a ball or read the paper. I finish at 4.30. You might not think so but its hard work and by knocking off time, I've had enough. Then I have to drive home, have a wash and I'm ready for something to eat. Doreen either makes me something if she's in or she leaves me something in the microwave. If she's working that's me sorted. I can't go out and I watch the box. Work, TV, bed, work. The kids more or less look after themselves until bedtime and, if Doreen's not in, I pack them off for the night. Whenever I do get the chance to get out I do. I think that is not much to ask in return for the years I've put in at work. I need something to take my mind off the bills, the job, the journey. My marriage is like everybody else's, more habit than anything, but I have done my best for them and I won't let them down.

Doreen: If it needs doing in our house, I have to do it. John's out all day and would be every evening if he could be. I do get a cup of tea in the mornings but I've yet to come in to a hot meal. I work three mornings a week on the tills at the local supermarket and three nights a week stacking shelves at a big chemists. I have to fit everything around my work, including the kids. They're very good but they don't get much of a look in, even at weekends. I'm not interested in going out in the evenings. I'm usually too tired to care! I work because we need the money. Every penny I earn is spent before I get it. I'm not interested in what passes for entertainment around here – clubs, pubs, bingo – plus the fact that I haven't really got anyone I could go out with. I don't know many of the people on the estate. The housework doesn't do itself in this house and I don't think I could tell you what 'free time' means. I like to listen to the radio when I'm ironing. I worry about the kids and what they'll do for a living when the time comes. As for me, I have no choice but to carry on carrying on. I do sometimes think of just walking away from it all and, when the kids have gone, I might. If there was ever any love in our marriage, its gone now. I need more than this.

understanding and fail to confer any positive regard for the client's cultural roots' (Gambe *et al.* 1992, p.26).

Such pathologising is ethnocentric (and racist) in so far as it gives 'privileged status to the world view or experience of the dominant ethnic group at the expense of other ethnic groups' (Gambe *et al.* 1992, p.22). In contrast to such deficit models of Black family functioning, Ratna Dutt (in Macdonald 1991, p.77ff.) has developed a model of practice which:

- recognises and values the real life experiences of Black people
- recognises what is implied in surviving racism
- is sensitive to cultural pride
- encourages and promotes the development of positive self images for Black children and families
- is based on a holistic approach to the family and their support systems.

It is perfectly possible to offer an account of the potential strengths of some Black families, although one might be reluctant to for fear of substituting one set of stereotypes for another. Such an account would include the fact that some families will include kinship ties that are much more extensive than in traditional White families. Such ties may extend across continents and time and be an invaluable source of support in times of stress. A Black family's sense of community may be much more positive and one's sense of personal identity may owe more to family and community than to the Western idea of 'rugged individualism'. Family patterns and the importance of blood ties, rather than, in some instances, marriage ties, may elevate the importance of inter-generational relationships above those more commonly found in White families and provide additional sources of support. There may be greater respect for the wisdom of elders and so on.

We repeat that we do not wish to imply a set of all-embracing Black cultural norms. Our purpose is to encourage you to reflect on your own potential to see Black families in pathological, deficit and racist terms and to:

'...build in a recognition of cultures of strength and resistance to racism into the mainstream of [your] social work theories and models. This is a necessary first step in the development of antiracist social work practice in the area of child and families' (Gambe *et al.* 1992, p.27).

A second major strand in the failure of social work to respond to the needs of Black families has been a reluctance to acknowledge the inadequacy of existing models of service delivery. Typically, practitioners and planners have adopted a 'colour blind' approach where Black service users are treated the same as White service users. Not only does this fail to recognise the specific experience of racism, it fails to take account of cultural and ethnic differences and strengths. In order to fully take account of the value of different cultures, histories and traditions, it may be necessary to treat people differently. For example, in relation to Black children who have to live away from home and be looked after by the local authority, the child's *particular* needs in relation to food, clothing, cosmetics, sense of cultural identity and sense of self as a Black child need to be taken fully into account.

Another familiar strategy for refusing to amend existing models and modes of practice is to place all of the responsibility for Black children and families on Black workers. This neatly makes Black people responsible for the consequences of racism and allows White workers to consider the needs of Black service users as someone else's problem.

Such techniques of avoidance are both cause and effect of the lack of strategic monitoring by the providers of social work services of the appropriateness, take-up and usefulness of their services to Black children and families. Consultation with actual or potential Black service users remains the exception rather than the rule and the active engagement of Black people in the management, planning and delivery of such services, rarer still. Beginning to see social work as part of the problem is the first step to making it part of the solution. It needs to be if we are to ensure that Black families' needs are better met and their legitimate entitlements are more fully secured in future years than they have been hitherto.

 **CONCLUSION**

Both as an idea and as a particular set of personal and social relationships, the family is a major organising principle in our lives. But, just as much as our lives are infinite variations on a single theme, so too are our ideas and experiences of the 'family'. The family is all of the things that this

Unit has described and much more besides. In this richness and variety lies the family's capacity to respond and adapt to the changing social context in which it continues to evolve. The death of the family has been much exaggerated. Because of its richness, variety and adaptability, the family satisfies many individual and societal needs. The only thing that the family is not is a fixed set of expectations and common experiences. It isn't even a demographic fact! As a social worker you will encounter the family in all its many and varied forms. You should celebrate its diversity rather than condemn its deviations from what you may have experienced, were expecting or might prefer to find.

NOTES AND SELF-ASSESSMENT

1. Where do you set the limits on who you count as 'family'?

2. Do you think that others might define your family differently? Who and why?

3. Are your relationships with members of your family fundamentally different to your relationships with other people?

4. Is your family a 'typical' family? Why/not?

5. What does the phrase 'to start a family' mean to you? Have you or do you intend to do so? Why/not?

6. What does the phrase 'family values' mean to you?

RECOMMENDED READING

Langan, M. and Day, L. (1992) (eds) *Women, Oppression and Social Work – Issues in Anti-Discriminatory Practice.* London: Routledge.

Macdonald, S. (1991) *All Equal Under the Act?* London: REU/NISW.

Elliot, F.R. (1986) *The Family – Change or Continuity?* London: Allen and Unwin.

TRAINER'S NOTES

Exercise 2.1: Family Fortunes

In a group setting, the questions can be put in the form of a quiz, following the pattern of any one of a number of TV game shows. Plotting individual answers on a chalkboard or flip chart can provide a graphic account of the range of answers that will be provided. Reviewing the results in this way (as though they were obtained by some kind of survey) is useful in encouraging a debate on the sources of people's (mis)perceptions without participants having to defend their own position or particular guesstimate. All of the answers are in the Study Text so we will not reproduce them here!

Exercise 2.2: Is this a Family?

A larger group can be broken down into smaller groups and answers compared in the usual way. A much more challenging (but safe) discussion can be engendered by having pairs take the position of the various putative families and argue their case with the larger group for their being accorded 'family' status. Some 'families' have an 'easier' case to argue so the larger group may need to be encouraged to range more widely in their reasons for denying such status, for example by considering communal forms of child care, such as kibbutzim, as more appropriate to *true* family life. At the end of the 'debate' the whole group should consider what difference it would make to the 'families' concerned whether they were accorded family status or not. Practical consequences, such as entitlement to state support, should be considered as well as more personal considerations, such as one's sense of identity and the degree of social in/exclusion that follows from recognition as a family.

Exercise 2.3: A Day in the Life

A similar approach to that used in Exercise 2.2 can be adopted here with group members 'taking sides' in a debate. However, it is important that the group should focus on the inter-relatedness of the conditions that impinge upon both John and Doreen and how adjustments in one area imply consequences in others.

UNIT 3
Parenting

OBJECTIVES

In this unit you will:

- Examine the nature of parenting and explore the core skills and tasks of parenting.
- Explore personal models of what constitutes 'good enough parenting' in the context of the Children Act 1989.
- Develop an understanding of the model of parental responsibility established by the Children Act 1989.

 **PARENTING**

Unit 1 explored the needs and rights of children and concluded that children both have needs to be met *and* they have rights to be honoured. They certainly have a need and a right to have someone around to look after them – someone to care for them during the period when they are unable to care entirely for themselves. In this Unit we will focus on parenting and explore what it involves and what it means to be a 'good enough' parent. For, whilst humans may be unique in choosing to be parents, to our knowledge no one has ever described parenting as either straightforward or easy.

The following Study Text illustrates how elusive any fixed sense of what we mean by parenting can be and begins with a consideration of what motivates people to become parents in the first place.

Study Text 3.1: Defining Parenting

It is not always clear what it is that motivates people to become parents. You may wish to speculate on why your parents had you. The sort of reasons which are usually advanced include:

- personal fulfillment
- to please a partner
- for immortality
- failed contraception
- to get housing
- to complete a family.

It is important to realise that parenting can be begun for purely selfish reasons but even if people choose to have children with the noblest of intentions, parenting is something that parents have an interest in too. Parenting is not something 'given' to children disinterestedly. The frustration of parental expectation is, in itself, often the cause of family dysfunction. Parents have needs and rights too, as well as an emotional stake in the relationship.

We make this point to remind ourselves that parenting can be understood more broadly than as a straightforward response to the needs and rights of the child. We have seen how childhood can be socially constructed to meet the needs of adults (Unit 1). It is useful to consider parenting in a similar way and as equally problematic. What passes for appropriate parenting varies over time and between different cultures just as fascinatingly as does childhood and family form. Before the Industrial Revolution in Britain, for example, parenting was more evenly shared amongst the wider family, along with much economic activity. Later, when paid labour was organised outside of the home, women increasingly became the primary care givers. Society's expectations of parents have also changed.

A good illustration of how parenting, and the expectations that are held for it, can vary over time can be found in a comparison of the advice given in parent manuals and baby care books. In 1946, for example, mothers were advised that:

'Babies and children are all the better for a little "wholesome neglect". From the beginning an infant should be trained to spend most of his time lying alone... Do not point things out to him' (Frankenburg 1946, p.171). Almost forty years later, parents were instructed: 'After love the next most important thing that you can give your child is stimulation. A small child is like a sponge soaking up practically every new idea and experience he or she comes in contact with. So, to be good parents, start introducing your child to the outside world' (Stoppard 1983, p.12).

Parenting also changes across cultures. It is very tempting to understand parenting only in the context of our own experience and our personal construction of family life. However, there is a danger in judging parents according to only one, often very restricted, standard. In some cultures, for example, child rearing is seen as the responsibility of the extended family, indeed of the whole community. Children may be praised and disciplined by others as well as by their parents. Children may have a number of role models to learn from and may have much greater involvement with their elders. In Oliver's account of a West Indian childhood: 'The children automatically look to all the grown-ups for comfort, guidance, treats, attention, punishment... If a child misbehaves it is as likely to be slapped by its cousins, sister-in-law or its next door neighbour as by its mother' (1979, p.143).

Just as the needs and rights of children do not determine or presuppose a single model of parenting, neither does any one culture or time in history presuppose a single mode and manner of parenting. Different ways of parenting are becoming more familiar if only because of demographic changes. As we saw in Unit 2, there is an increasing number of one-parent families who have chosen to bring their children up alone, for example.

In establishing the principles of good practice that underpin the Children Act 1989, the Department of Health made the point forcefully:

Although some basic needs are universal, there can be a variety of ways of meeting them. Patterns of family life differ according to culture, class and community and these differences should be respected and accepted. There is no one perfect way to bring up children and care must be taken to avoid value judgments and stereotyping. (DOH 1990a, p.7)

One useful way of thinking of parenting that does not imply a particular household structure, class or cultural origin (but which still carries particular assumptions about the nature of childhood!) is to de-construct it into its constituent parts and imagine it as a job like any other. That is the function of the next exercise.

Exercise 3.1: The Job of Parenting

TASKS:

1. Using the proforma on the next page, devise a job description for a parent.

2. Design a simple advertisement for the job.

3. Design a selection process so that the right person gets the job.

Points to Consider

1. Is this a 'post' that is best job shared? If so, how?

2. What working environment would best suit this job?

3. What prospects of career development are attached to this post?

4. What training is most appropriate for this job?

5. Are the rewards commensurate with the duties?

6. Is it a job that you would ever consider taking on? Why/not?

JOB DESCRIPTION and PERSON SPECIFICATION
Post: Parent
Hours: . . . . p.w.   **Salary:** £. . . . . . p.a.   **Annual leave entitlement:**
Responsible to:
Responsible for:
Main areas of activity:
Qualifications required:
Previous experience required:
Personal qualities required:

Figure 3.1 Parenting job description

PARENTING SKILLS

Whilst it might be amusing to think of parenting in the way that you might think of paid employment, the comparison is an instructive one. In terms of the commitment of time and effort, parenting would stand comparison with almost any job, of course. But thinking of it in this way might also have prompted you to consider how, like many other jobs performed primarily by women, it is undervalued, exhausting and highly skilled. Just how skilled a role it is, we shall explore in the following exercise.

Exercise 3.2: Core Skills of Parenting

TASKS:

1. Make a list of skills needed to parent a child of 0–10 years.

2. Make a list of skills needed to parent a child of 10–18 years.

3. Compare both lists and underline similarities and note the differences.

4. Identify the core skills of parenting.

Make sure that you concentrate on skills, not on qualities – that is patience may be needed but it is a quality. The skill lies in how a parent actually copes with the behaviour of the child requiring patience; for example, by the use of non-verbal skills, listening skills or the ability to switch off!

Points to Consider

1. How well does your list of parenting skills fit your map of children's needs constructed in Exercise 1.2?

2. Which parenting skills (if any) come 'naturally'?

3. If not by nature, where or how do you think people acquire the appropriate skills for parenting?

4. Is it likely that any one individual or couple will possess *all* of the skills that you have identified as being appropriate to the tasks of parenting?

5. Is it possible to teach particular parenting skills?

6. If it were, what skills would be required by the person providing the training?

GOOD ENOUGH PARENTING

It might be argued that there are certain skills involved in being a parent that operate irrespective of the particular culture in which a child is being brought up, the particular point in history through which s/he lives or how many people are involved in the task of parenting. These focus on meeting the primary needs of a child and which help to establish a child's self-esteem and social identity.

It would seem, however, that few people are likely to be able to be in possession of all of them, certainly not at the beginning of their parenting career. How then do we settle for less than the ideal, given the importance we attach to the process of parenting? The following Study Text examines what is meant by 'good enough' parenting.

Study Text: 3.2: Good Enough Parenting

Pugh and De'Ath (1984) include the following in their formidable list of parental attributes: 'the ability to love, care, support, communicate, make decisions, cope with stress, a flexibility of mind, consistency of attitudes and behavior and practical skills' (p.18).

Parents not only provide physical care but they show affection, stimulate, discipline and reward their children. They also socialise them and give them room to become independent. The hours are long and the pay can be very poor indeed. And so far we have only considered the core skills of parenting. Some parents may need additional skills; a Black parent, for instance, will need to teach her child to counteract racism. We would argue that skills can be learnt and practised and simply because they *can* be learnt, examined and measured they are open to analysis, understanding and, most importantly of all, to intervention by social workers. However, we must recognise that certain structural conditions may prevent a parent from developing, maintaining or exercising those skills. Poor housing, unemployment and poverty add to the stress of child rearing and may limit a person's ability to parent adequately. Most parents, at some time, will be too worried about making the money stretch to the end of the week to remember to praise and encourage their children. There are some obvious and some unexpected delights in being a parent but it can be a difficult job, not least because it seems to demand so much of parents in terms of basic skills. It should not be surprising that parenting cannot always be maintained at the highest level or that it sometimes breaks down altogether. So, if perfect parenting is unachievable, what might constitute 'good enough' parenting?

The phrase 'good enough parenting' was coined in 1965 by D.W. Winnicott in his book *The Maturational Process and the Facilitative Environment*. For Winnicott, good enough parenting was where parents provided what he described as a 'facilitating environment' that permitted each child to have her or his needs met and potential developed. It meant parents adapting their behaviour and life-style as far as possible for the child's well-being rather than their own and for parents to put their child's needs first in all major family plans and decisions. Although this account of good enough parenting might be considered today to represent a counsel of perfection, the term clearly implies that there is no such thing as simple, undiluted *good* parenting. It implies that no parent can meet her/his child's needs all of the time and that it will be important to find a balance between their own needs and those of their children. The Children Act 1989 is said to recognise that parents are individuals with needs of their own and that social work has an important part to play in supporting parents in their care-taking role:

> ...parents are entitled to help and consideration in their own right. Just as some young people are more vulnerable than others, so are some mothers and fathers. Their parenting capacity may be limited temporarily or permanently by poverty, racism, poor housing or unemployment or by personal or marital problems, sensory or physical disability, mental illness or past life experiences. Lack of parenting skills or inability to provide adequate care should not be equated with lack of affection or irresponsibility. (DOH 1990a, p.8)

'Good enough' parenting also implies that parenting is situational, that several different forms of parenting can be good and that there is no single universal model across class and cultures.

Clearly, however, the term also implies that the parenting still needs to be good. If a child is abused or rejected, the parenting is clearly not 'good enough'. How do you, as social workers, come to recognise and be able to articulate where your threshold of tolerance of 'good enough' parenting stands? In part, your judgment will arise from your understanding of the needs and rights of children and from a realistic assessment of what is involved in parenting. Part of your judgment, however, will be based on your own untested assumptions, attitudes and values. The next exercise is intended to provide you with the opportunity of examining the foundations of your own judgments of 'good enough' parenting.

Exercise 3.3: Good Enough Parenting

TASKS:

1. For each of the following five scenarios, rank the parenting on a scale from 1 to 5 (1 = good enough; 5 = totally unacceptable).

2. Identify very clearly on what basis you have reached your decision.

   1. Jim and Sue have three children under five. They have just won first prize in a national lottery and decide to put their three children up for adoption, buy a boat and sail around the world. It is something that they both dreamed of doing before they had children. All three children are adopted by a childless couple who could never have had their own children.

Good Enough   *1   2   3   4   5*   *Totally Unacceptable*

---

   2. Liz is a single parent living in a damp twelfth-story flat. She has two children: Sarah, aged 9 and Tom aged 5. The youngest one is still in nappies, even Sarah still wets the bed at night. She is rarely in school or seen out playing. Liz says that she needs to keep Sarah at home to help look after Tom and to mind the flat, especially if Liz has to go out to the shops, as she is scared that the flat would be broken into again if left unoccupied. Sarah is Liz's only company, according to Liz. She has suffered several attacks on the house.

Good Enough   *1   2   3   4   5*   *Totally Unacceptable*

---

   3. Mary had Jason, now aged two, when she was 17 years old. Alan, Jason's father, is 22 and lives with Mary and Jason. Mary says that Alan is too strict with Jason and won't let her pick him up if he cries at night or even play with him when Alan is around. Mary says that this is partly Jason's own fault as he is very demanding and does wear her out. 'He has never been a good baby, like other people's'. She has been to the doctor to

get something to make Jason sleep at night. 'Things were OK between Alan and me before Jason was born'.

| Good Enough | 1 | 2 | 3 | 4 | 5 | Totally Unacceptable |

4. Pete and Steph are solicitors with busy, high-profile practices. Pete is often abroad for long periods. Steph works long hours. Sophie, the youngest child, aged four, is collected daily from play-school and spends the afternoon at her childminder's house. In the evenings, Mrs Evans, a qualified Nanny, puts Sophie to bed and reads her a story. Pete and Steph's other two children are at boarding school. During the holidays Pete and Steph take the children on exotic holidays. At the weekend, the children, if at home, go to the cottage that the family have in Norfolk, usually with Mrs. Evans.

| Good Enough | 1 | 2 | 3 | 4 | 5 | Totally Unacceptable |

5. Sian has been in prison three times for shoplifting since the birth of her children. Bill, her husband, takes off for long periods 'working away'. The three children of her marriage, aged 3, 5 and 7, have all been fostered on several occasions, separately and together. Bill's idea of helping at home is to smack the children if they are naughty. He says this is a hard world and the children have got to learn to stand on their own two feet and the sooner the better. Sian refuses to do all the cooking and washing. 'Why should she?' she says, 'Bill doesn't do anything'. There are lots of arguments between Sian and Bill. The children often have to fend for themselves.

| Good Enough | 1 | 2 | 3 | 4 | 5 | Totally Unacceptable |

If you find it difficult to come to a decision, you may wish to examine each scenario more closely by means of the 'Parenting Profile' grid (Figure 3.1) and consider how each example of parenting meets the different needs of a child and then calculate an average score for the purposes of comparison.

Needs of child	Good Enough		Totally Unacceptable		
	1	2	3	4	5
Physical care					
Affection					
Security					
Stimulation of Innate Potential					
Control					
Guidance					
Development of Independence					
Valuing and					
Respect					
(Development of Self-identity)					

Figure 3.2 Parenting profile

Points to Consider

1. Do parents have to be 'good enough' in all areas or is it sufficient to be only 'good enough' in most?

2. Does being 'good enough' in one area compensate for not being good enough in others?

3. How might a child's view of 'good enough' parenting differ from that of an adult?

4. Is the lack of 'permitting circumstances' sufficient to excuse not 'good enough' parenting?

5. Is your parenting or that which you received as a child 'good enough'? Why/ not?

5. Is your parenting or that which you received as a child 'good enough'? Why/ not?

6. Is the term 'good enough' a meaningful tool for a social worker to use when coming to a decision about the care of a child? Is it too crude or too vague?

 **RESPONSIBLE PARENTS**

The research on parenting, whilst it may have focused more on particular family forms thought to be problematic, is nonetheless consistent in outlining the essential features of good parenting:

> Absence of conflict, even when parents are divorced or separated, reliably providing physical care and comfort, consistently demonstrating love and affection, the ability of parents to see the child's point of view, setting clear limits but paying more attention to good behaviour than to bad and much praise and little criticism are all likely to prove beneficial to the child. Spending time with children and engaging in enjoyable activities with them is important too. (DOH 1996, p.6)

Several of the scenarios in Exercise 3.3 suggested that one further aspect of 'good enough' parenting is the balance struck between the needs and rights of the child and those of the parent. You probably found it fairly easy in the first scenario to recognise that the balance was far from right. In scenario 4 the decision is a little less straightforward. If the two carers had less glamorous occupations and their economic circumstances were a little less comfortable, the balance might be said to have shifted. In scenario 2 the situation is altogether more complicated.

Given that the Children Act 1989 (the Act) is sometimes (wrongly) referred to as the Children's Act and, like every other piece of childcare legislation in modern times, is frequently described as a 'children's charter', one might anticipate that the law has come to favour the child's case over the parent's – in a way that D.W. Winnicott might have warmly endorsed. In fact, the situation is much more complex. The position of parents in law has been clarified through the introduction, in the Act, of the very important concept of 'parental responsibility'. The next Study Text provides a technical account of what is meant by parental responsibility and the final Study Text in this Unit relates parental responsibility to a wider consideration of parenting and the law.

Study Text 3.3: Parental Responsibility

INTRODUCTION

Somewhat illogically, the Children Act 1989 (the Act) defines the concept of parental responsibility only after it has established how it is allocated or acquired. To avoid confusion, we have chosen to do much the same. However, you may wish to note the formal definition of parental responsibility provided by the Act as a preliminary to a brief explanation of its distribution. Section 3(1) of the Act defines parental responsibility as: 'all the rights, duties, powers, responsibilities and authority which by law a parent of a child has in relation to the child and his property'.

DISTRIBUTION AND ACQUISITION OF PARENTAL RESPONSIBILITY

Not all parents have parental responsibility, as defined by the Act, for their children. Similarly, not everyone with parental responsibility for a child will be the birth parent of that child. Certain categories of person have parental responsibility as of right and others can acquire it. Indeed, more than two people can hold parental responsibility simultaneously. This may all seem very odd at first, but if we consider parental responsibility as primarily concerned with matters concerning the upbringing of a child, it will be clear that parenting can easily be shared with others besides a child's biological parents.

A child's mother always has parental responsibility for a child until the time of the child's majority, death or adoption. This applies whether the mother was married or not and even if anyone else, including a local authority, also has parental responsibility (although see below and Study Text 10.1 for how the exercise of parental responsibility is affected by the making of certain court orders, e.g. a care order).

A child's father will have parental responsibility, as of right, only if he was married to the child's mother at the time of the birth or if he subsequently marries her or if, by other statute, the child is deemed to be legitimate. The unmarried father does not have parental responsibility unless he actively seeks to acquire it. He can do this in a number of ways: by adopting his child, by being appointed the child's guardian upon the death of the child's mother, by formal agreement with the child's mother under s.4(1)(b) (which can only be brought to an end by order of the court) (s.4(3)), by obtaining a parental responsibility order (s.4(1)(a)) or by virtue of a residence order made in his favour. If a residence order is made in favour of an unmarried father, then the court must also make a parental responsibility order which may survive the residence order.

A step-parent (i.e. someone married to a child's parent), provided that the child was treated as a child of the family, may obtain parental responsibility by adopting the step-child or by obtaining a residence order in respect of the child. The parental responsibility attaching to a residence order which is not in favour of a child's parent or guardian specifically excludes the right to consent (or withhold consent) to adoption or to appoint a guardian (s.12(3)). The parental responsibility attaching to all residence orders also excludes the right to change the child's name and the right to take the child out of the UK for more than a month unless the court or all those with parental responsibility agree (s.13).

A local authority can obtain parental responsibility upon the making of a care order (see Study Text 10.1). The parental responsibility attaching to a care order specifically excludes the right to determine the child's religion, to appoint a guardian, to free for adoption, to change the child's surname and to arrange the child's emigration (s.33). Although the making of a care order does not extinguish the parental responsibility of anyone else (except those who hold parental responsibility exclusively by virtue of a residence order), it does give the local authority the power to determine how far others may exercise their parental responsibility. A local authority may also acquire parental responsibility (as would *any* applicant) upon the making of an emergency protection order. This is a very restricted form of parental responsibility directly concerned with the emergency protection of the child.

The other category of person who can obtain parental responsibility is someone appointed to act as a child's guardian after the death of the parent(s) who made the appointment (s.5).

Everyone who has parental responsibility for a child may act independently unless the consent of others with parental responsibility is
specifically required or unless the court has prohibited the exercise of an
aspect of parental responsibility. Consent to a child's marriage requires the
consent of all of those with parental responsibility (Marriage Act 1949,
s.3). If a residence order is in force, all parental responsibility holders must
agree to the child's name being changed or to the child being taken out
of the UK for more than a month (s.13). The consent to a child's adoption
requires the consent only of the biological parent(s) with parental responsibility (Adoption Act 1976, s.16).

MEANING OF PARENTAL RESPONSIBILITY

The Act itself does not develop or illustrate what is meant by 'parental
responsibility' beyond the rather general definition noted above. When
originally formulated, the intention was to provide sufficient flexibility in
the law to meet the changing needs and circumstances of children (see
Guardianship and Custody, Law Commission 1988, No.172, para.2.6).
However, the courts have given consideration to various aspects of
parental responsibility. These include, as we might have anticipated from
the foregoing, the power or duty to:

- determine a child's religion
- determine the child's education
- name the child
- appoint a guardian for the child
- consent or withhold consent to medical treatment for the child
- consent or withhold consent to the child's marriage
- represent the child in legal matters
- consent or withhold consent to the child's adoption
- lawfully correct the child
- arrange the child's emigration
- protect and maintain the child
- administer the child's property
- have the physical possession of the child
- have contact with the child.

The legal arrangements for most of these have already been described but we would wish to comment further on three aspects in particular: the rights/powers to consent or withhold consent to medical treatment for the child, to lawfully correct the child and to protect and maintain the child.

CONSENT TO MEDICAL TREATMENT

A person obtaining the age of 16 is able to give or withhold consent to their own medical treatment, surgical, medical or dental, including any diagnostic process or test. Below that age, the decision is dependent upon whether: 'the doctor considers [the child] of sufficient understanding to understand the consequences of consent or refusal' (DOH 1991a, para.2.32). This determination, which follows an important decision in the *Gillick* case (see Study Text 3.4), sets an important condition upon parental responsibility in that it clearly indicates that the exercise of parental responsibility is mediated by the child's developing competence.

LAWFUL CORRECTION

Section 1 of the Children and Young Persons Act of 1933 establishes that it is an offence to assault, ill-treat, neglect or abandon a child (under 16) in such a way as might cause unnecessary suffering or damage to health. However, section 1(7) of that Act states that: 'Nothing in this section shall be construed as affecting the right of any parent…to administer punishment to him.' It is, therefore, a legitimate defence to a charge of assault upon a child to show that what was done was done by way of lawful correction. The correction must not be excessive either in kind or quantity. Corporal punishment is unlawful in children's homes, foster placements or state schools. Some would regard it as anomalous that it can continue in private homes.

PROTECTING AND MAINTAINING THE CHILD

Besides the duties imposed by the 1933 Act to do no unnecessary harm, there is a common law duty on any person who is looking after a child to protect him or her from physical harm by providing the 'necessities of life' (*R v Gibbins and Proctor* (1918) 13 Cr. App R 134). Given the powers held by virtue of the right to lawfully correct a child, you might be surprised to find the positive duty to look after a child expressed in such meagre terms.

We will return to examine some of the broader themes that emerge from an understanding of parental responsibility in Study Text 3.4 but in order to make sure that you fully understand parental responsibility, as defined by the Children Act 1989, you should try the following exercise.

Exercise 3.4: Parental Responsibility

Answer 'TRUE or FALSE'.

1. A child's birth father always has parental responsibility for his child.

2. A child's unmarried mother always has parental responsibility for her child.

3. Stepfathers, if they simply marry the child's mother, will have parental responsibility for that child.

4. Once parents are divorced, only the mother retains parental responsibility.

5. A brother or sister of a child cannot have parental responsibility for that child.

6. A specific issues order carries parental responsibility with it.

7. A residence order carries parental responsibility with it.

8. An emergency protection order does not carry parental responsibility with it.

9. A local authority can never obtain parental responsibility for a child.

10. The local authority can never interfere with the exercise of a mother's parental responsibility.

11. There is no limit to the number of people who can have parental responsibility for a child.

12. Once you have parental responsibility you can never lose it.

You can check your answers with those given in the Trainer's Notes at the end of the Unit.

Study Text 3.4: Children, the Law and Public Policy

At several points during this Unit we have raised the question of the balance between the legitimate interests of parents and those of children. This Study Text considers that balance further and raises another important question of balance: that between the interests of the parents and the interests of the state.

In considering whether to make a care or supervision order, and in certain other circumstances (s.1(4)), the court is required to consider 'the ascertainable wishes and feelings of the child' (CA s.1(3)(a)). This reference to the wishes and feelings of the child could be construed as evidence of the way in which the Children Act in particular, but also the law more generally, is moving towards an increasingly 'child-centered' approach in family matters.

We have indicated already how 'the courts have come to regard parental responsibility as a collection of powers and duties which follow from being a parent and bringing up a child, rather than as rights which may be enforced at law...[the term parental responsibility] more accurately reflects that the true nature of most parental rights is of limited powers to carry out parental duties' (DOH 1989, p.9). In this light, 'parental responsibility' can be understood as a responsibility *to* children and young people.

This point of balance can be seen to follow a series of precedents in the courts. Dewer (1992), for example, draws attention to Lord Denning's judgement in 1970 that the legal right of a parent '...is a dwindling right which the courts will hesitate to enforce against the wishes of the child, the older he is. It starts with a right of control and ends with little more than advice' (Per Lord Denning in Hewer v. Bryant [1970] 1 QB 357). This statement was one notable watershed in the changing balance of power between parents and children. More frequently cited is the judgement by Lord Scarman in the 'Gillick' case, in which the principle was established that 'parental right yields to the child's right to make his own decisions when he reaches a sufficient understanding and intelligence to be capable of making up his own mind on the matter requiring decision' (Per Lord Scarman in Gillick AC 112 at 186). We have already noted how this decision has had profound effects on a child's capacity to give or withhold consent to medical treatment.

There are other ways too in which the Act would appear to strengthen the position of children in relation to decisions taken about them. For example, a young person aged over 16 may consent to the provision of accommodation for him or herself irrespective of the wishes of his/her parents (S.20(11)) and the local authority is required to consult the child concerned when any decision is taken about him or her if s/he is looked after by the local authority (S.22(4)).

However, it is possible to see this shift in the balance in the relative power of parents and children to make decisions as standing in direct contradiction to another central theme of the Act, namely the stress that the Act lays on the primacy of the family. The family, especially the family of origin, is central to the operation of the Act, and much other social policy, and to any real understanding of the concept of 'parental responsibility'. The Children Act is officially described as resting 'on the belief that children are generally best looked after within the family with both parents playing a full part and without recourse to legal proceedings' (DOH 1991e, para 1.5). As Section 17 of the Children Act makes clear, it is now the duty of every local authority towards 'children in need' 'to promote the upbringing of such children by their families' (Children Act 1989, s.17 (1)).

We will see in Units 6 and 9, in the context of child abuse and child protection, that the interests of children and their parents may not always be congruent and that too often the family's interests are seen to be expressed exclusively in the adult's actions, attitudes and interests.

The apparent conservatism of the Act in this regard would seem to reflect the particular conservatism that produced not only this Act but which also froze Child Benefit and changed the Social Security rules to penalise young people living away from home. This is to see the Act in the context of what McCarthy has called the 'new politics of welfare'. In McCarthy's account, these politics offered:

> ...to reduce expenditure and shed responsibilities;...(they) would strike a curiously populist chord, finely tuned to the Thatcherite emphasis on freedom, self help and responsibility, which would

enable tens of thousands to 'give something back' to their own local communities by participating in social support. (McCarthy 1989, p.43)

In this context the family would have an important role to play. It would be the family that would serve 'in the front-line of care' (ibid., p.43), not just for children but for older people, people with disabilities and those with mental health problems. In this way the Children Act 1989 is to be seen as a close ideological relative of the later NHS and Community Care Act. But we have already noted how family form is changing and that the boundaries around the legal concept of marriage are becoming less distinct. Hence, it is parenthood that is increasingly being regarded as 'for life' in statutory terms:

[if] the bonds of parenthood are now assuming the degree of indissolubility once accorded to marriage, any significant readjustment in the relationship between the parents themselves and between parents and children is just as deserving of regulation as the dissolution of marriage itself. (Eekelaar 1991, p.173)

In establishing the concept of 'parental responsibility', the Children Act can be seen as doing just that. The parental responsibility of married parents can be ended only by death or adoption and the state will never assume exclusive parental responsibility for a child. The law will permit the concept of parental responsibility to extend to 'non-marriage' partners. Even where the birth father does not assume parental responsibility as defined by the Act, his role in maintaining the child financially cannot be escaped following the provisions of the Child Support Act 1992. Understood in this sense, the concept of 'parental responsibility' is not to be understood as simply implying that parents are responsible to their children, it implies also that parents are responsible for their children.

There can be few who would take issue with the idea that parents have particular duties towards their children and that they should have the necessary rights to fulfil those duties. But, in any given social context, the question arises of whether the rights and duties of parents, children and the state are properly balanced. Does the current balance imply that the family can enjoy greater security from intrusion by the state? Does it imply that they will have to rely more on their own resources to meet their family needs? Does it imply that, in the privatised family, parental authority is strengthened? Are the interests of children as well protected in law as those of parents?

These are not simply interesting theoretical points. These are precisely the boundaries that you will negotiate, as a social worker, every day of your working life.

CONCLUSION

There can be little doubt that parenting is a demanding and highly skilled occupation. We have concentrated rather more on the 'performance' aspect of the role in order to broaden your appreciation of just what is involved in the 'flesh and snot' realities of parenting. We hope that you will appreciate more sensitively the myriad opportunities there are for parenting to go awry and that you will recognise that a parenting-skills approach can be a useful way into improving borderline or 'not good enough' parenting. Besides being a collection of skills and a range of practical tasks, parenting is also a set of affective relationships and we will explore some of the complexities and subtleties when we consider separation and loss in Unit 5.

Beyond this, parenting is also an idea and an ideology. It is an idea that is used to establish the boundaries between the social worker and the families who receive a social work service and between the interests of parents and children. These are dynamic boundaries which, by negotiating in your professional role, you will also help to shape.

NOTES AND SELF-ASSESSMENT

1. Is parenting a full-time occupation?

2. Does everyone have a right to be a parent if they choose?

3. What obligations do parents have towards their children and vice versa?

4. How would you assess the parenting that you give/have received and how does this experience affect the judgements you might make of others' parenting?

5. Are the criteria that you would apply in order to judge parenting in your own family the same as those that you would use for the families with which you will work?

6. How good a parent would/ do you make?

RECOMMENDED READING

Adcock, M. and White, R. (1985) *Good-enough Parenting.* London: BAAF.
Pugh, G., De'Ath, E. and Smith, C. (1994) *Confident Parents, Confident Children: Policy and Practice in Parent Education and Support.* London: NCB.
Leech, P. (1994) *Children First: What Our Society Must Do – And Is Not Doing: For Our Children Today.* London: Michael Joseph.

TRAINER'S NOTES

Exercise 3. 1: The Job of Parenting

Group discussion, after comparisons of job descriptions, can focus on whether, on the basis of the advertisement, anyone present would apply for the job. This should allow a focus on the benefits as well as the disadvantages of being a parent, for example the first words, the first nativity play or special religious occasion. Role playing 'interviews' for the job allows participants to review the kind of reasons that people give for wanting children and can give rise to a discussion on when people 'should' have children and on who 'should not'. A lively discussion is the surest way of encouraging participants to reflect seriously on their understanding and preconceptions about parenting.

Exercise 3.2: Core Skills of Parenting

Divide participants into two groups: one to consider the skills needed to parent a child of 0–10 and the other the parent of a child 10–18 years. Make sure both groups can see each others' 'results' and go through them quickly, underlining similarities and debating differences. Then ask both groups to identify some core skills and to consider whether these are universal for every culture, country, religion, era in history, etc.

Exercise 3.3: Good Enough Parenting

Ask participants to work in pairs to rank the parenting on a scale of 1–5, identifying very clearly on what basis they have reached their decisions. Feedback by recording the range of scores for each scenario. This usually makes the point that the assessment of parenting, based on the same facts, will vary substantially from person to person (social worker to social worker).

You may wish to go a stage further and explore in more detail some of the reasons on which people based the scores they gave. This can be done in open discussion or by asking groups to reconcile widely varying scores and not to let them out until they agree!

It is also possible to explore the different scores by reference to the Grid. Using a different colour for each scenario, take feedback from the participants. Discussion should centre on the value base for awarding a ranking on each of the criteria. Try and get a consensus and mark the point on the scale. When each of the aspects of the child's needs have been addressed, join up the markings, thus making a profile. Do this for each scenario. You will see different shaped profiles emerging.

Exercise 3.4: Parental Responsibility Quiz

Answers: 1. False. 2. True. 3. False. 4. False. 5. False. 6. False 7. True. 8. False. 9. False. 10. False. 11. True. 12. False.

Supporting

OBJECTIVES

In this unit you will:

- Examine the statutory basis on which support services to children and families are provided.
- Explore the range of support services available to children in need.
- Explore what is meant by 'partnership practice'.
- Consider the application of partnership practice to the provision of support services.

 **SUPPORTING CHILDREN AND FAMILIES**

Unit 3 concluded with an appreciation of the demands of parenting. As a child grows, the skills required and the resources needed to parent effectively continue to change and develop. Both child and parent mature and their personalities, expectations and needs alter with the passage of time. There are any number of points, especially in the changing context of child rearing practice and family formation, where relationships can go awry. Similarly, circumstances can be such that effective parenting is made even more exacting. Racism, low income, ill-health and poor housing can make an already difficult job almost impossible. Particular children may also present particular challenges. Some 360,000 children and young people aged under 16, 3 per cent of the UK child population, have disabilities (OPCS 1989). Such children may require even more of their parents and carers in order to achieve their potential and to make the most of their childhood. It is hardly surprising that most, if not all, parents and children need help with the business of growing up and getting on at some time or other. Social work with children and families is substantially about the provision of such help.

Clearly, not all families who need help become the subject of social work interest or intervention. We have seen already (Study Text 3.4) how the Children Act 1989 regards the family as the primary context for the care of children. It is important to recognise how recently the question has arisen of how, or even if, there should be formalised and systematic services to help support families through the processes of parenting. The first half of this century bore the indelible mark of deeply humiliating and publicly shaming Poor Law provision. Writing about the state of the law in 1947, S. Clement Brown reminds her readers how the legacy of the preceding age found legislative echo in her own time:

> Some of our laws still express the view that our duty to the homeless child ends when we have fed and clothed him and trained him in habits of soberness and industry. The duty of the local authority in respect of destitute children, beyond giving them 'relief', is still only to 'set (them) to work or put (them) out as apprentices,' though they are empowered in the cold words of the Act [Poor Law Act 1930, S. 15, 53–57] to establish separate schools for 'the relief and management of the children to be received therein'. (p.iii)

Prior to the implementation of the Children Act 1989, the local authority's role in providing services to those children and families not subject to a specific statutory order was largely limited to the direct prevention of reception into formal care or receiving the child into care on a voluntary basis under the grounds established by the 1980 Child Care Act (substantially a re-enactment of the 1948 Act, about which Clement-Brown was writing in the extract quoted above). This particular form of care allowed the possibility of the local authority assuming 'parental rights' over a child and potentially excluding parents from any future substantial involvement in the child's life. Thus parents and family members who had asked for some specific help from social workers because they were unable to care for their children, for example through illness, bereavement or stress, could find themselves handing over control of their children much more substantially than had ever been intended.

The Children Act 1989 is said to mark a radical shift from the Poor Law-derived practices of the recent past where statutory agencies in particular, but social work generally, confined their activities to providing the lowest level of services consistent with protecting the child from harm without feeling under any particular obligation either to work constructively with parents or to maximise a child's life-chances or potential. In contrast, the Children Act 1989 is said to enable families to 'look to social services for support and assistance. If they do this they should receive a positive response which reduces any fears they may have of stigma or loss of parental responsibility' (DOH 1991b, para.2.14). As such, the Act implies not only a degree of flexibility in how support services might be delivered but it implies also a different relationship between the providers of services and their users. This Unit will describe the statutory basis for social work practice to support families requiring help and explore the concept of partnership practice as it relates to the provision of support services. It begins with an account of the terms used in the Act to identify who might be eligible to receive such services.

Study Text 4.1: Children in Need

Part III of the Children Act 1989 establishes the local authority's duty to provide an appropriate 'range and level of services' for certain children with the aim of 'safeguarding and promoting' their welfare and, so far as is consistent with that aim, to do so by promoting 'the upbringing of such children by their families'. (s.17 (1)). The children concerned are those which the Act describes as 'children in need'.

The definition of a child 'in need' is to be found at s.17 (10). A child is in need if:

(a) he is unlikely to achieve or maintain, or to have the opportunity of achieving or maintaining a reasonable standard of health or development without the provisions for him of services by a local authority under this Part;

(b) his health or development is likely to be significantly impaired or further impaired, without the provision for him of such services; or

(c) he is disabled.

'Development' means physical, intellectual, emotional, social or behavioural development and 'health' means physical or mental health (s.17 (11)). A child is 'disabled' if he or she is 'blind, deaf or dumb or suffers from mental disorder of any kind or is substantially and permanently handicapped by illness, injury or congenital deformity'. This definition of disabled is the same as that contained in the National Assistance Act 1948 and so a person with disabilities qualifies for services both before and after the age of 18. The Act makes allowances for services to be provided for a child's family, or any member of the child's family as well as to the child itself, if these are provided 'with a view to safeguarding or promoting the child's welfare' (s.17 (3)). Family is widely defined to include 'any person with parental responsibility for the child and any person with whom he has been living' (s.17 (10)). This definition of need is deliberately wide in order to re-enforce the Act's commitment to provide services across a broad range. Local authorities cannot exclude any category nor can the definition of 'need' be restricted only to those children at risk of significant harm.

Direct services for children in need will not only be provided by local authorities, however. The local authority is required to 'facilitate the provision by others' of support services (s.17 (5)). So, even if you are employed in the voluntary or independent sector, your work may derive from the provisions of Part III of the Act. The local authority is required to 'take reasonable steps to identify the extent to which there are children in need within their area' (Sch.2, para.1(1)) and to publish information about the services that they provide, or which are provided by voluntary or other organisations, in such a way as those who might benefit from them are informed (Sch.2, para.1(2)). They are also required to open and maintain a register of children with disabilities in their area (Sch.2, para.2(1))

In order to determine whether a particular child is a child 'in need', the Act acknowledges that some form of assessment will be required

(Sch.2, para.3). Such an assessment may be carried out as part of a wider assessment of special needs. Guidance and Regulations (DOH 1991d, para.2.5) make it clear that such an assessment should be wide-ranging yet focused:

> In assessing individual need, authorities must assess the existing strengths and skill of the families concerned and help them to overcome identified difficulties and enhance strengths. Sometimes the needs will be found to be intrinsic to the child; at other times, however, it may be that parenting skills and resources are depleted or under-developed and thus threaten the child's well-being.

Guidance (DOH 1991d, para.2.7) proceeds to emphasise that assessments should reflect the spirit in which support services are to be provided:

> Good practice requires that the assessment of need should be undertaken in an open way and should involve those caring for the child, the child and other significant persons. Families with a child in need, whether the need results from family difficulties or the child's circumstances, have the right to receive sympathetic support and sensitive intervention in their family's life.

In particular, assessments and services should take account of the particular needs of the child in terms of education, religious persuasion, racial origin, cultural and linguistic background and the appropriateness of the agency providing or intending to provide a service (DOH 1991d, para.2.8).

As well as in relation to children in need, the Act also confers some other duties upon local authorities to provide support services. The authority is required, through the provision of services under Part III of the Act, 'to prevent children within their area suffering ill-treatment or neglect' (Sch.2, para.4). It is also required to take 'reasonable steps' to reduce the need for care proceedings, criminal proceedings against children, to encourage children within their area not to commit offences and to avoid the need to place children in secure accommodation (Sch.2, para.7).

Ultimately, the determination of a child as a child in need will be the consequence of the professional skill and judgement exercised by social workers. The next Exercise is intended to re-enforce your understanding of how the Act forms the context for those decisions.

Exercise 4.1: In Need?

For each of these mini case studies decide whether the child concerned is a child in need as defined by the Children Act 1989 and write down as precisely as you can how the child satisfies the criteria established in Part III of the Act.

1. Sharen is 15 and pregnant. She fully intends to look after her baby herself, with the help of her mother. Sharen currently shares a bedroom with her sister, aged 11. Her two brothers and her parents occupy the other bedrooms in her semi-detached house. Her mother seems reconciled to the facts of Sharen's situation but her father is angry and upset and refusing to speak to Sharen. Tension between family members is rising and there are frequent arguments between various members of the family.

2. John, age 4, lives with his mum and older brother, Ian, in a council maisonette on a very large estate on the outskirts of a major city. Mum survives on social security benefits but she is in debt (for about £500, used to buy a cooker) to a money lender. John has few clothes and no winter coat. Food is not very nutritious but he never goes hungry. There are only a few toys in the home and the local playground has been vandalised.

3. Mark, aged 14, has been involved with others in petty theft in and around his home area. He has not yet come to police attention officially but his family are concerned that this will only be a matter of time. Mark's parents are teachers and live in one of the better parts of town. Neither Mark or his family are happy with the slowly deteriorating state of family relationships that is occurring as a consequence of rows over Mark's behaviour. Relationships have always been good up to now. When Mark's father heard that his son had been truanting from school he telephoned the social worker saying that he had had enough and that something had to be done.

4. Robbie is aged 12. He is a keen supporter of the local football club and likes to dress in imitation of his heroes. Recently the club

changed their first-team kit and Robbie now wants to buy a replica shirt and a suitable (and expensive) pair of trainers. He says that he has been excluded by his friends at school because he is dressed so badly and that he will soon have no friends left if he cannot keep up with them.

5. Sanjit is the lone parent of Ayse, aged 3, who has severe learning difficulties and some mobility difficulties. Ayse can do very little for herself and requires almost constant attention. Sanjit is finding the physical demands on her exhausting. Ayse's father was killed in a traffic accident and she and her mother have no other friends or family in the area. Sanjit works in the local launderette part-time where she can take Ayse but she often feels lonely and at the end of her tether.

6. Mr Smith is having an affair with the wife of a family friend. He has been out of work for several years, despite numerous offers of work. Mrs Smith knows all about Mr Smith's affair and makes no secret of her contempt for her husband. Despite the fact that the family are in severe financial difficulties, both Mr and Mrs Smith have extravagant tastes and substantial credit card debts. The Smith's son, Jamie, is aged 8. He is a very timid boy who has recently started to wet the bed at night. His bed is already ruined and Mrs Smith has asked you to help.

Points to Consider

1. What factors did you take into account when determining whether the development of the child concerned was at issue?

2. What factors did you take into account when determining whether the health of the child concerned was at issue?

3. How did you decide what was a 'reasonable standard' of health or development?

4. What factors did you take into account in deciding what 'significantly impaired' might mean in each case?

5. In your decision making, did you accord more importance to the particular characteristics of the child concerned or to the circumstances in which they found themselves?

6. Was the degree of responsibility or culpability of the parents an issue in deciding whether each child was a child in need?

A RANGE OF NEEDS AND SERVICES

Once the determination has been made that a child is in need of services it will be for the local authority, in partnership with other agencies, to make suitable provision for the child concerned. Study Text 4.2 sets out how the Act requires or permits certain forms of support service.

Study Text 4.2: Services for Children in Need

The Children Act 1989 (the Act) requires local authorities to make available the following services for children in need:

- advice, guidance and counselling
- occupational, social, cultural or recreational activities
- day care or supervised activity
- home help
- travel assistance
- assistance to enable the child to have a holiday
- maintenance of the family home
- financial assistance
- accommodation.

The local authority must provide or facilitate the provision by others of *advice, guidance and counselling* as well as *occupational, social, cultural or recreational activities* for all children in need living with their families (Sch.2, para.8). Such services may also be provided for other children not in need. Often such services will be available via family centres which the local authority is required to provide under the Act (Sch.2, para.9). The nature and level of services offered by family centres varies enormously. Gibbons, Thorpe and Wilkinson (1990) have distinguished three main types of centre: the client-focused centre, where users are mainly referred by statutory organisations; neighbourhood centres, which have a more open-door policy and more flexible staff roles; community development orientated centres, which are managed by local people and concentrate on providing self-help groups rather than facilities for casework. The most common form is the neighbourhood family centre, which aims to combine some individual support with running advice groups for parents and day care facilities for children. Guidance (DOH 1991b, para.3.20) differentiates between centres in a similar way and identifies therapeutic centres, where skilled workers carry out intensive work with families in extreme difficulty; community orientated centres, which families might use as a meeting place and to take part in activities; self-help centres, where services might be offered in a very informal, unstructured way.

Day care, which includes day nurseries, playgroups, toy libraries, out-of-school clubs and holiday play schemes must be provided for all children in need aged five or under (if not in school) and may be provided for other children too (s.18). The local authority has no power or duty under the Act to make provision for *home help, travel assistance* or *holidays* other than for children in need (Sch.2, para.8). Where a child in need is living away from home (but is not being looked after by a local authority), the local authority must take steps, if necessary, to promote the child's welfare, to enable the child to *live with its family* and/or to promote contact between the child and its family (Sch.2, para.10).

In exceptional circumstances, not defined by the Act, the local authority may offer assistance in *cash*. Any service offered, excluding advice, guidance or counselling, may be subject to a charge to the service user (s.29 (1)).

The local authority must provide *accommodation* for a child in need who requires accommodation if:

- there is no one with parental responsibility for him (s.20 (1)(a))
- he is lost or abandoned (s.20 (1)(b))

- the person caring for the child is prevented from providing the child with suitable accommodation, for whatever reason and whether permanently or not (s.20 (1)(c))

- the child is over 16 and the local authority considers that the child's welfare is likely to be seriously prejudiced if accommodation is not provided (s.20 (3)).

Accommodation provided in this way is dealt with at greater length in Unit 5 but it should be noted at this stage that when a child is accommodated under the provisions of Part III of the Act, the pre-existing distribution of parental responsibility is unaltered. The local authority does not acquire any parental responsibility for the child, although it does acquire certain duties and obligations to safeguard and promote the child's welfare (s. 22 and Study Texts 5.3 and 8.2).

 MAKING CHOICES

It is important to recognise that 'need' is not an absolute or unitary concept; there are different kinds and degrees of need and a variety of ways of meeting it. The choice of appropriate response is rarely unconstrained, however. Often the social work task, in the context of insufficient resources to meet demand, is that of balancing the competing claims made by different groups or individuals, each of which has a legitimate case to make. It should be remembered also that just as certain kinds and degrees of need have higher or lower claims on an agency's resources, so it is also the case that certain forms of support service are more acceptable to some groups than others.

Consider for a moment how the parents of children with disabilities might feel at having their child included on a register maintained by the social services department. Some may welcome the formalising of social services support but others may be offended by being associated for the first time with people who require social work intervention. They may regard a social worker's visits as stigmatising and far less acceptable than having a health visitor call. Others may regard the supply of services by a voluntary agency as the equivalent of receiving charity. The following exercise will further illustrate the point.

Exercise 4.2: Providing a Service

Return to the mini case studies used in Exercise 4.1.

1. Rank order the case studies from the highest level of need to the lowest.

2. List which services you feel may be appropriate to those children whom you have identified as being in need. You may refer to the services already mentioned in the Unit and any other you may be aware of from your own experience.

3. Consider how acceptable such services might be to the person who would receive them and to their carers.

4. Now be realistic and, from your experience and knowledge of the current services in your locality, note how likely it would be that services could be delivered in the way that you have indicated.

Points to Consider

1. What factors did you take into account in determining levels of need?

2. Do you think that the concept of the child 'in need' is a helpful one in determining how to prioritise service responses?

3. Other than the level of need, what else is likely to influence the nature and level of service responses?

4. In your experience, which kinds of services are least likely to be stigmatising?

5. Imagine that you are the parent of a child with a disability. You have heard that the local authority are opening a register for children with disabilities. What information would you be happy for social workers to collect?

6. What do you understand to be the primary purpose of providing support services to families?

 **A NEW ALLIANCE?**

It should be clear that the supply of support services is a contingent process; not all families who have difficulties will be defined as 'in need', not all families who are eligible for services will receive them and not all of those who are eligible and who could receive them will choose to do so. Any reluctance to engage with social work support services, especially those supplied by the local authority, may be coloured by a sense of their Poor Law heritage. However, there is ample research evidence to suggest that a great deal of child care practice has, in the recent past, been characterised by a persistent mutual mistrust on the part of the recipients and the providers of such services that is of much more immediate origin.

Three important reports issued by central government since 1985 have argued consistently for a better working relationship between the families of children in difficulties and social workers. The first of these, *Social Work Decisions in Child Care – Recent Research Findings and their Implications*, (DHSS 1985) noted in its foreword that: 'Sensitive and knowledgeable work by professional social work practitioners is required to secure a practical partnership with parents which will operate in the best interests of the children.' The report went on to argue for the need to 'consult, inform and work *with* parents' (p.20) and to urge (p.22): '...shifts in attitude[s] and priorities, increased understanding, more sensitive perception of client's feelings by social workers...'.

The second report, *Patterns and Outcomes in Child Placement – Messages from Current Research and their Implications*, (DOH 1991c) located the barriers to 'practical partnership' in tradition and bureaucracy, in the lack of skill, sensitivity and time available to social workers, the nature of parents own problems and in problems over the balance of power (p.44) and noted that: 'None of these characteristics offers an easy basis for reciprocal trust between parents and social workers and the latter will need to take initiatives and work hard to build a genuine partnership.'

The latest report, *Child Protection – Messages from Research*, (DOH 1995a, p.86) in a section called *Paternalism or Partnership?* found 'a clear link between better outcomes for children and greater involvement of parents' and added that (p.87): 'All family members stressed the importance of being cared about as people. They could understand that the professional had a job to do and that procedures were necessary, but they strongly objected to workers in whatever profession who did not appear to listen, did not show warmth or concern or who only did things by the book.'

The consistent message of all three reports is one of developing new alliances between the users and providers of services (between social workers and their 'clients') and between differing service providers. This idea has been captured in the term 'partnership' which, as you would now expect, proves to be yet another social work chimera. The following Study Text will sensitise you to some of the broader currents of thought that influence contemporary ideas of partnership practice in child care in preparation for the final Exercise in this Unit, which provides an opportunity to consider partnership in the context of the provision of support services.

Study Text 4.3: Partnership Practice

PARTNERSHIP, POWER AND ANTI-OPPRESSIVE PRACTICE

At the heart of any discussion about the nature of partnership practice lies the question of power. In its everyday sense, the idea of a partnership implies a set of power relations that tend towards equality and mutuality. The *Shorter Oxford English Dictionary* defines a partner as: 'one who is associated with another or others in some business, the expenses, profits or loses of which he proportionally shares – a husband or wife – a companion in a dance – a player associated on the same side with another'. If we add to this definition, which tells us more about where partnerships take place than anything about the idea itself, some of the assumptions we make about these settings, we can infer that a partnership:

- extends over time
- is for better or worse, richer for poorer
- involves shared aims
- involves a degree of mutual adjustment, like the partners in a dance.

However, there is a power inherent in the role and status of social workers, particularly, but not exclusively, when operating in a statutory context that tends towards the opposite of what is implied in the dictionary definition, away from mutuality and reciprocity towards an imbalance of power in favour of the social worker.

The power possessed by the social worker derives from a number of sources, not least legal mandate and societal expectation (Davies 1994). It derives also from the possession of specialist knowledge and skills (Johnson 1972). There is a sense in which this is inevitable and certainly the assumption is deeply embedded in the social work literature and in contemporary practice. When the particular constellations of negative values that have hitherto characterised social work thinking (its euro-centricity and its gender biases for example) are considered, many would agree that in relation to understanding oppressive practice of whatever sort, the issue of power, its sources and its uses are central.

Phillipson has noted that understanding the uses and abuses of power 'is crucial to social work because social work needs to work with a framework for understanding those elements that are embedded in oppression and its repercussions' (1992, p.14). Individual practitioners may often feel that they have very little power. It is true, as Phillipson suggests, that there are structural dimensions to sexism, racism and other forms of oppression that are less amenable to the actions of any individual. Even, at a more mundane level, if you work in a large bureaucracy, strategic decisions over the allocation of scarce resources, for example, may appear to be taken at some remove from you. But, just as there are structural dimensions to oppression, so too are there personal ones. We have indicated already how 'gatekeeping' (facilitating access to existing services) often revolves around particular professional judgements in specific cases. The point at issue is not how much power social workers have or where else in society power is located. The point at issue is *how* the power that *is* possessed by social workers is used, either exclusively to impose definitions or assessments of problems or inclusively to enable or empower others. This is central to any understanding of the principle of partnership practice and the provision of support services to children and families. In so far as partnership is based on a commitment to genuine mutuality, reciprocity, negotiation and the prospect of a real alliance, it is a form of practice that can give real substance to a commitment to anti-oppressive practice.

THE POWER OF PARTNERSHIP

It will not always be the case that power can be shared equally between social worker and service user. Sometimes this would not even be desirable. Partnership practice is not a form of utopianism but can make power differentials explicit and productive rather than covert or denied. But, as with all partial solutions, partnership practice also has the potential to be its own contradiction and to legitimate the existing structure of power relations. Coit (1978), writing about partnership in the context of community development, illustrates how partnership can be conservative:

- 'partnership' at a local level tends to mask structural inequalities and class antagonisms
- 'partnership' encourages compromise and conciliation in order to obtain minimum concessions
- 'partnership' is operated by professionals
- 'partnership' weakens local leadership.

Indeed, common sense would suggest that partnership can easily be corrupted since it is essentially about power sharing. Few ever give up power willingly. It may be more helpful to conceive of degrees of partnership – some more cosmetic than others – to see partnership operating along a continuum determined by the nature of the power relations.

Arnstein (1972) has described a general progression that begins at one end of the spectrum with 'manipulation', where it is only the worker who knows the rules, can diagnose the problem, pronounce upon the cure and determine whether it has been achieved. One degree better than this is 'informing', where the service user is paid the courtesy of being told what will happen to them next. Then comes 'consultation', when the voice of the other is heard but is by no means necessarily heeded. Then 'placation', where Coit's 'minimum concessions' are won. Then on to 'partnership' itself, which still falls short of what Arnstein calls 'delegated power', where, for example, a budget might be delegated and then, finally, on to 'citizen control' and the New Jerusalem. (For alternative continua of partnership see Cox and Parish 1989 and Butler 1996b).

THE VALUE OF PARTNERSHIP

Partnership practice ultimately should be judged by its achievements, how it helps children and families deal with the problems with which they are confronted. For the population at large, partnership is valued for what it helps one achieve, its instrumental value. For the users of social work services it is not to be valued only for how it makes one feel, its expressive value. If it has real value, partnership practice must have sharing as its determining characteristic; shared purpose, a sharing of knowledge, expertise, information and skills and a sharing of resources, power and decision making. Partnership is more than a means to an end in that it implies a significant change in the philosophy and practice of many social workers. Atherton and Dowling (1989) offer a statement of values which lie at the heart of partnership practice that many would find challenging;

- Partners trust each other. So they can be open and honest in how they behave to each other. They try to understand rather than to judge.

- Partners respect each other. There is complimentarity rather than equality where the special skills and knowledge of the worker are made accessible to the client in the way that has been negotiated with the client.

- Partners are working towards the same broad objectives.

- Partners share power. Nobody has a monopoly on it and nobody takes over. That power may never be equal but it should be possible for the balance of power to shift by negotiation and agreement.

- Empowerment of the client can be assisted by ensuring that the views of each partner carry weight and are respected and by sharing information.
- Partners share in decision making.
- Partners can call each other to account and have rights. Partnership practice does take the issue of accountability seriously and provides for any partner to call for explanations and challenge what work is going on.

Exercise 4.3: Partners?

This Exercise is based on the first of the mini case scenarios used in Exercise 4.1. and the worst kind of social work response that can be imagined. Read the additional material set out below and complete the tasks which follow.

> Sharen's mother contacted the health visitor in order to see what kind of support might be available. She had hoped that the family might be able to obtain some practical help around the house when the baby was born and that the doctor might be able to write in support of an application to the housing authority so that the family could eventually move to a four-bedroomed house.
>
> Later that day a social worker called to see Sharen. It soon became clear from the line of inquiry being pursued by the social worker that the matter was being viewed as a 'child protection' issue, although it was not clear whether the child concerned was Sharen or her baby. Sharen had told the social worker who the father of the child was and had been informed that this may prove to be a matter for the police as Sharen was 'under age'. The social worker told Sharen that her school had already been contacted. Sharen had not told anyone outside of her family up to this point as she was not entirely sure what she wanted to do concerning her future plans. Sharen became very upset. The social worker told her that regular visits would be required from that point on as Sharen did

not seem to be emotionally capable of looking after herself, let alone her child. Sharen's mother asked the social worker to leave and was informed that it would be in the family's interest to allow such visits as 'there was always the possibility of going to court'.

TASKS:

1. 'Quickthink' all of the potential support services that could have been made available to Sharen and her family.

2. Consider how Sharen and her family are likely to view any help that the social worker, health visitor or other professional is now able to offer them.

3. Consider how the response made will influence the likelihood of Sharen or her family asking for help in the future

4. Describe an appropriate response by the health visitor and the social work agency.

 **Points to Consider**

1. In what sense and to whom are the professionals in this case accountable for their response? To whom should they be accountable?

2. How might Sharen and her family's objectives differ from those of the professionals involved? What might be the points of conflict?

3. Why might the social worker not trust Sharen and her family to know what help they want?

4. Who *should* be making the decisions in this case? Who will?

5. Is it realistic to think of partnership practice in the context of a potential child protection issue?

6. What are the limits of partnership practice?

CONCLUSION

In considering how families might best be supported through the difficulties that they encounter, we have suggested that the value and usefulness of that support and its appropriateness and acceptability are in some measure dependent on the terms on which it is offered. We have suggested that partnership approaches have a potential for establishing the kind of relationship best suited to helping families deal with their problems. Partnership practice depends on a willingness on the part of the social worker or other professional to think about their role in relation to families in difficulty quite differently to how they have done in the past. In turn, this requires a thorough appreciation of what personal qualities and professional style social workers bring to the helping relationship. It has been known for a long time that the characteristics of social workers that service users most value are:

> ...honesty, naturalness and reliability along with an ability to listen. [They] appreciated being kept informed, having their feelings understood, having the stress of parenthood accepted and getting practical help as well as moral support. (DHSS 1985, p.20)

> Social workers are experienced as helpful if they really listen and take pains to understand the difficulties from the family's point of view. They are also valued if they are practical as well as sympathetic and supportive and do more than just listen. Honesty and directness are important qualities that parents are well able to appreciate – even if some messages are hard and unpalatable... (DOH 1991c, p.47)

> Honesty and reliability were particularly valued. Clearly presented information about what was happening and the options available were both very important. (DOH 1995a, p.46)

This is not a counsel of perfection. It is what is needed to do the job, assuming that the job is one of helping families resolve their difficulties.

NOTES AND SELF-ASSESSMENT

1. Why provide support services to children and families?
2. To whom do you regard yourself accountable in the exercise of your professional duties?
3. Do you trust the users of social work services?
4. In your working relationships with families, do you prefer to lead or to follow?
5. How well do you take guidance?
6. Is your practice characterised by 'honesty, naturalness and reliability along with an ability to listen'?

RECOMMENDED READING

Daines, R. *et al.* (1990) *Aiming for Partnership.* Barkingside: Barnardos.

Family Rights Group (1991) *The Children Act 1989: Working in Partnership with Families.* London: HMSO.

Gibbons, J. *et al.* (1990) *Family Support and Prevention: Studies in Local Areas.* London: NISW.

TRAINER'S NOTES

Exercise 4.1: In Need?

This exercise can be undertaken using an 'objective' needs checklist. A matrix, based on the terms of the Act, could be developed in discussion and without reference to the cases. Participants could refer back to the material generated in Exercise 1.2 or 3.3 for ideas on what to include in the matrix. This matrix could then be tested on the six cases and the points at which it 'failed' could be the basis for a critique of the Act's definition of 'in need'. Groups may tend to focus rather more on the scarcity of resources than on the right to privacy and freedom from interference by the state when it comes to looking at an appropriate social work response. Participants should be encouraged to explore what limits there should be on the state's role in supporting children and families.

Exercise 4.2: Providing a Service

Task 1 can be undertaken as a kind of 'balloon debate'. A scenario could be imagined in which resources are particularly scarce and only one case will receive any services at all. Each case study is represented by one or more members of the group, who have to argue the merits of their case and persuade other group members that their case should be the one to receive services (in a balloon debate proper, the participants have to imagine that they are in a hot air balloon that is slowly descending as it loses air. In order to stay aloft, participants have to jettison, in turn, one member of the balloon's company until only one person remains).

Task 3 can be undertaken as a 'dreams and nightmares' exercise. Half of the group is asked to imagine the worst possible way in which a particular service (from the list generated at Task 2) could be delivered. For example, day care could be provided in a vandalised building with untrained staff with convictions for child abuse, etc. The second half of the group has to imagine the perfect way in which such services could be delivered. Day care could be provided for free in a well-equipped building by caring staff who are all well qualified, etc. Then views are contrasted and a sense of what is practical and desirable established, as well as a possible action plan as to how the particular service could be developed.

Exercise 4.3: Partners?

This exercise works well as a role play or as another 'dreams and nightmares' exercise. Participants should be encouraged to see the 'nightmare' response as capable of 'making sense', assuming a particular view of the role and tasks of social work. Participants should be prompted to see the internal logic of the response made in this case, which has a certain plausibility and to recognise those characteristics in their own practice that would tend towards such an authoritarian, 'expert' response.

UNIT 5
Looking After

OBJECTIVES

In this unit you will:

- Learn about attachment and separation.

- Explore current issues in the care of children looked after by the local authority.

- Consider the provisions of the Children Act 1989 in relation to looked after children.

- Reflect on what is best practice in relation to looking after children.

 LOOKED AFTER CHILDREN

We noted in Study Text 4.2 that the provision of accommodation was included in the range of services made available to children in need by the Children Act 1989. We shall go on to learn (Unit 10) how a child may be received into the formal care of the local authority by virtue of an order made in court. Both groups of children, those provided with accommodation on a voluntary basis under Part III of the Act and those placed in the care of the local authority at the direction of the court, are described by the Act as 'looked after children' (s.22(1)) and it is looking after in this specific sense of the term that is the focus of this Unit.

Any episode of being looked after away from home begins with an experience of separation. This is frequently a painful process that makes enormous demands on the emotional and personal resources of everyone involved. Whilst this is no more than a statement of the obvious, it has, on occasions, been forgotten in practice as the following extract from the Clyde report of the inquiry into events on Orkney makes clear:

> Mrs. B had got up as usual between 6.15 am and 6.30 am in order to wake WB[1] at about 6.50 am in time to catch the school bus. On this morning she had gone out to the caravan[2], woken WB and gone back to the kitchen. Then she heard the noise of cars outside the house... The Police approached and knocked on the front door. When Mrs. B appeared they then explained their presence. Mrs. B responded by shouting at them and the social workers were called over... WB had woken up before the police and social workers arrived. She emerged from the caravan in a dressing gown obviously distressed and stood in tears held by her mother in the confined space formed by the side of the caravan and the front wall of the house. Mrs. B grabbed her and hugged her, shouting observations to the social workers to the effect that they were evil, that they were not taking the children and why could they not let her prepare the children... The social workers attempted to calm her and encourage her to return to the house. While they were so engaged she led WB to the porch and WB slipped into the house, went upstairs and locked herself in the bathroom. Two police officers and a social worker followed her upstairs... (Clyde Report 1992, paras. 6.10/11)

Whilst we make no comment on the causes of the social workers' concerns for the 'B' children or on the subsequent conduct of the case, the anguish and desolation of 'WB', made all the more awful by the detached manner in which her experience of separation is described, is almost unbearable. It is important that we begin any consideration of looked after children with an appreciation of the enormity of what separation, including much

---

1   A girl, aged 13.
2   The caravan, where WB slept with her sister, was kept in front of the family home.

less traumatic ones than that of WB and her mother, can mean to a child and its parents. The following Study Text provides a brief account of attachment theory as a prelude to an Exercise that is intended to sensitise you to the emotional and broader psychological impact of separation.

Study Text 5.1: Attachment, Separation and the Looked After Child – the Work of Vera Fahlberg

ATTACHMENT

Vera Fahlberg, in the introduction to her book *Fitting the Pieces Together* (1988), expands on Kennell, Voos and Klaus's (1976) definition of attachment as 'an affectionate bond between two individuals that endures through space and time and serves to join them emotionally' and goes on to note that:

> A strong and healthy bond to a parent allows a child to develop both trust in others and self reliance. The bond that a child develops to a person who cares for him or her in their early years is the foundation of their future psychological, physical and cognitive development and for their future relationships with others (p.13).

Attachments form the basis of our later psychological integrity and our capacity to engage in rewarding and reciprocal social and emotional relationships. Bonding is the process by which attachments are made. It starts before birth when a parent forms mental images of the new infant and begins to develop expectations and hopes for its future. From the moment of birth onwards, bonding proceeds as a consequence of a mutually reinforcing cycle of events that is part of many routine parent/child interactions. These interactions involve touch, sound and visual stimuli appropriate to the child's stage of physical and cognitive development. A typical successful interaction might occur, for example, when an infant is hungry or uncomfortable. S/he shows this by moving or crying. While in this state, the infant is unable to perceive anything else of the world. Their carer notices and accurately meets the need or satisfies the child. The child feels better, is quietened and content. The parent is gratified by the response. The infant is able to perceive the world around them again and subsequently becomes aware of further needs and so the cycle continues, as in Figure 5.1. It is not only the child who might initiate these positive interactions, so too might the carer(s). For example, in the case of an infant, the carer might 'coo' or talk to the child which may elicit a smile which encourages the carer to 'talk' more and so on.

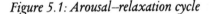

Source: Fahlberg 1988, p.25

Figure 5.1: Arousal–relaxation cycle

There are many reasons why the bonding cycle may not be initiated or might be disrupted. It may be that the carer is not attached to the child for reasons relating to the nature of the pregnancy or the circumstances in which the child was conceived. Alternatively, it may be that the baby may have been born prematurely or with some medical condition that prevents the parent from entering into the child's routine care on a regular or sufficient basis for the virtuous circle described in Figure 5.1. to develop.

Fahlberg (1985) notes the several deleterious effects of lack of normal attachment. These include: poor development of conscience, poor impulse control and lack of foresight, low self-esteem, poor interpersonal skills and relationships, lack of emotional awareness and sensitivity, reduced cognitive ability and some general developmental problems such as poor verbal skills and difficulty in aural comprehension. One should note, however, that Fahlberg has been criticised (see Gambe *et al.* 1992, p.29 ff.) for the euro-centricity of her views in that she moves from a 'universal concept of attachment to a context bound view' which emphasises the importance of a primary caretaker and the child's developing sense of autonomy. This does not take into account different cultural patterns of child rearing which may involve multiple caretaking and a more positive evaluation of inter-dependency over individualised autonomy. Practitioners will need to be wary of drawing negative inferences from differing patterns of attachment within a particular family or cultural context.

SEPARATION

The separation of a child and its carer can occur for many reasons and it is important to understand normal reactions to separation. Bowlby (1970) cited in Fahlberg (1988) described three stages which the child goes through when separated from a person to whom they are particularly attached:

- the child complains strongly and makes attempts to go and find the absent carer
- the child despairs of recovering the carer, but continues to be watchful. The child may appear pre-occupied or depressed during this phase but when a car drives up or there is a voice at the door, the child becomes alert, hoping that the absent carer is returning
- the child becomes emotionally detached and appears to lose interest in the absent carer.

These behaviours, which, it should be stressed, are perfectly normal reactions to separation, can vary, according to Fahlberg (1988 p.40), depending on:

- the nature of the child's attachment to the primary caretakers
- the nature of the primary carers' bonding to the child
- the child's past experiences of separation
- the child's perceptions of the reasons for the separation (especially whether they view themselves as responsible)
- the circumstances of the move itself
- the environment to which the child is moved
- the environment from which the child was moved.

SEPARATION AND THE LOOKED AFTER CHILD

It will often be the case that looked after children will have had less opportunity in the past to form strong attachments, particularly if their childhood is characterised by family breakdown or successive moves within the care system. However, given that the function of attachment behaviour is ultimately self-protective, both physically and psychologically, it may be the case that the prospect of enforced separation may come to represent sufficient threat to force a child into reliance on what limited attachments they do have. Hence a child may well cling to an abusive parent and exhibit hostility to the worker, who, in such circumstances, may represent the greater threat. Where normal prior attachments do exist, workers must be careful not to misinterpret reactions to separation. It is not uncommon for children to react aggressively during separation and to apparently lose interest in their former carers or the prospect of a return home as part of the normal self-protective response.

The importance of the separation experience to the subsequent process and outcomes of intervention cannot be underestimated. In a review of the research literature on admissions to residential care, Bullock, Little and Milham (1993) concluded that the 'secondary problems' associated with 'separation and strained relationships' 'can so preoccupy the child and his or her carers that the primary problems necessitating the child's removal from home are neglected... Indeed, the problems separated children experience as they try to preserve the continuity of their personal and family relationships may overwhelm any benefit that might reasonably be expected to accrue' (p.16).

 Exercise 5.1: Separation

Re-read the account of the removal of the 'B' children from their parents quoted in the introductory Course Text for this Unit.

1. Using your imagination and your own personal experience of separation, write a 250 word account of the experience from WB's point of view (we would stress that you are not being asked to try to recreate what happened during the actual removal of the 'B' children or to imagine what she might have felt. You are being

asked to imagine how *you* might have responded in similar circumstances). In particular, think about and describe:

- how you might have felt at the moment you awoke
- what you might have thought was happening
- what you might have wanted to do as soon as you were awake
- who you might have wanted to talk to
- who you might have wanted to be with
- what you might have felt as you heard the sound of other people's distress
- where you might think you were being taken
- what you might think would happen to you next
- when you might think you would see your bedroom or house again
- when you might think you would see your family again.

2. Make a list of all of the steps that could have been taken that might have eased the experience that you have just described.

Points to Consider

1. In circumstances such as those described in Exercise 5.1, in what ways might the experience of separation be different for the parent of a child and the child itself?

2. How might the experience for parent and child be different if the separation is at the request of one of them rather than at the insistence of someone else?

3. What might be the long-term effect of a traumatic separation on the child's and/or the parent's relationship with the worker(s) or agency implicated in the separation?

4. What might be the emotional cost to the workers involved in the separation of a child and its parent(s)?

5. What strategies, both productive and unproductive, might workers, parents and children adopt to protect themselves from the confusion and pain of a traumatic separation?

6. Is it possible to take all of the pain and confusion out of any enforced separation?

 SPECIAL PESSIMISM

Later in this Unit (Exercise 5.3), and as part of Unit 8 (Exercise 8.2), you will have the opportunity of considering how to ameliorate the effects of separation. At this point we wish to maintain a broader focus as we explore current issues in the care of looked after children. The following Study Text concentrates on residential care in particular, although we do address the imbalance that this creates in Exercise 5.2, which focuses on foster care. We have placed the emphasis on residential care for a number of reasons. First, popular and professional interest in residential care has been more intense during the 1990s than for many years previously. Recent accounts of how children are actually looked after have often made sad reading. In recent years the name of Frank Beck has become almost as well known as that of Jasmine Beckford. In Staffordshire, North Wales and Northumberland particular children's homes have attained national notoriety for the way in which children have been abused at the hands of those who have been entrusted with their care. Consequent public and professional concern has resulted in centrally-driven initiatives in the development of practice (e.g. The Support Force for Children's Residential Care) and in social work training. Accordingly, we expect the challenges facing residential care to remain firmly on the social work agenda for the foreseeable future.

Second, the fact is that much more research has been undertaken into residential care than into most other forms of care provided for looked after children and our knowledge base is accordingly a little more sound in this area than in others. This is not to say that the available research is particularly current or that it is comprehensive. There are some notable gaps, particularly in relation to the effects of the Children Act 1989 on practice and outcomes (see Bullock, Little and Milham 1993, pp.22–23).

The third reason is a more personal one. It is our experience that field social workers and other professionals tend to undervalue, or even discount, residential care as a learning resource whilst in training and, more importantly, they tend to disregard residential care as a viable resource in practice. Few become engaged in the continuing debate about the role, function and future of residential care. This is a wide-ranging and important debate encompassing attitudes and values as well as substantial changes in the population of looked after children and in the range and type of provision available. We begin the Study Text with a consideration of some of the negative attitudes to residential care that are commonly encountered.

Study Text 5.2: Residential Care and Looking After Children

ATTITUDES TO RESIDENTIAL CARE

> Virtually all social workers appear to view admission to care very negatively. They see it as a last resort and as a sign of failure to prevent the break up of families. They are also worried about what the care experience will do to children and parents. Residential care is looked on with special pessimism. (DHSS 1985, p.46)

The origins of this special pessimism can be traced to a number of sources. The progenitors of many residential establishments were the Poor Law workhouses where conditions were intended to be such as would discourage the feckless and their children from making demands on the parish. Young people are still able to articulate both the stigma and the punitive air that can characterise the experience of being looked after:

> You know there's a lot of parents of kids in care who use a kind of threat. 'I'll 'phone the welfare and they'll take you away'. This automatically gets identified in the public mind with a place of punishment, doesn't it?

> Being in care you feel you've got a cross on your back. You feel marked. (NCB 1983, pp.16–17)

More recently, in the 1950s, an appreciation of the consequences of institutional care generally (e.g. Goffman 1961) and the particular contribution of John Bowlby, whose work was, in part, based on observations of the inadequacies of the care given to infants in residential nurseries, further undermined the foundations on which the smoke-stained stones of the nineteenth-century workhouse and the high walls and open spaces of the reformatory or cottage home were built.

Over the last thirty years, increasing concern about the quality of care provided for looked after children and young people, rising costs, a growing practice and policy interest in preventive strategies – given particular impetus by the 1963 Children and Young Person's Act and a marked (but not entirely defensible) preference for foster care (see Butler and Owens 1993) – have led to an almost continuous review and revision of residential care.

More immediate anxieties about residential care at the start of this decade where identified by Utting (1991, p.23) as follows:

- the falling number of residents and residential places raising questions about the future role and place of residential care in an overall child care strategy

- an associated loss of a sense of direction, purpose and esteem amongst the providers and users of residential services

- an awareness of gaps in local authorities' policies and inadequacies in the management of residential care

- the staffing of residential units was over-weighted with unqualified and inexperienced workers

- the changing nature of the population of residents posing problems of care and control.

Moreover, the status of residential care in professional terms has long been bound up with the low status of caretaking generally. As 'women's work' (see Study Text 2.2), looking after children is regarded as unskilled labour – a fact which continues to be reflected in the pay differential and disadvantageous terms and conditions of residential social workers.

THE CHILDREN

There have been significant changes in the population of looked after children over recent years.

These broad indicators mask particular shifts in the population of looked after children in residential care. For example, 70 per cent of those in residential care are aged over 13 compared with only 42 per cent for the whole population of looked after children. The older a child is at the point of admission, the more likely s/he is to be placed residentially (35% at age 11 rising to 50% at age 17) (Utting 1991, p.28). A slightly higher proportion of those looked after in residential care are boys. Moreover, research (Rowe, Hundleby and Garnett 1989) would suggest that residential services are having to accept 'more difficult' young people, although the diversity of the residential child care population must also be acknowledged.

THE ROLE AND FUNCTION OF RESIDENTIAL CARE

Both as cause and consequence of the changing population of looked after children, the role and function of residential care has, over recent years, been called into question. The Wagner Committee (1988), in its review of residential provision aimed at enabling 'the residential care sector to respond effectively to changing social needs' (p.1) identified five areas in which there was a continuing role for children's residential provision (p.96). These were:

- respite care: e.g. to enable 'natural and foster families to continue to care for their disturbed or handicapped members'

- preparation for permanent placement: e.g. to provide a 'structured, caring, nurturing environment linked with a realistic plan' for children for 'what are hoped to be lasting arrangements for them'

- keeping families together: e.g. sibling groups

- care and control: e.g. for 'a small minority of children identified as a risk to themselves or others'

- therapeutic provision: e.g. for 'socially and emotionally damaged children'.

Table 5.1: Looked after children

	1982	1994	Change
Number of children looked after by local authority	88,663	49,000	-39,633
Sex of looked after children (B/G)	59/41	53/47	-/+6%
Age of looked after children (% under 10)	29%	36%	+7%
Proportion of looked after children in residential/foster homes	58/42%	38/62%	-/+20%
Proportion of looked after children subject to care orders	55%	58%	+3%
Staff employed in community homes	20,510	11,449*	-9,061

Figure is for 1993

Sources: DOH (1995b) *Children Looked After by Local Authorities 14th October 1991 to 31 March 1993 England.* London: DOH/ Government Statistical Service and DOH (1996) *Children Looked After by Local Authorities Year Ending 31 March 1994 England.* London: DOH/ Government Statistical Service.

Based on the characteristics of the existing population of looked after children, Utting (1991, p.33) suggests an equally broad ranging taxonomy of residential care as the best or preferred option when:

- containment and treatment in secure accommodation is required
- children have decided that they do not wish to be fostered
- children have had repeated bad experiences of foster care
- intra-familial abuse has occurred such that placement with another family is undesirable
- there is a need for sophisticated and expert treatment
- children from the same family need to be kept together.

Issues of how such a multiplicity of functions can be carried out within any particular arrangement of residential units, or within any particular management or administrative structure, lie beyond our current interest but problems of differentiation and of the integration of residential care with the broader strategic aims of child care services are matters of current debate (see WO 1991; DOH 1990b; DOH 1991d, paras.1.16–1.26).

THE PROBLEMS OF THE CORPORATE PARENT

In the light of prevailing attitudes and in the context of so much change, the difficulties of providing an adequate service have been many and are well known. A series of central government-sponsored research programmes in the 1980s (reported in DHSS 1985; DOH 1991c) noted *inter alia* that:

- social work attention fades once a child is in care for any length of time

- children in care experience many changes of placement

- leaving care is not usually the result of any social work planning

- little attention is paid to maintaining the child's relationships with its own family

- parents of children in care feel excluded and many are disillusioned.

We saw in Unit 3 how difficult and demanding the job of parenting can be, even where it is based on parental love that is 'partisan, unconditional, does not cease, does not have cut off points, is long suffering and does not evaluate' (Parker and Milham 1989). No public body can replicate this and at the heart of the difficulties faced by the corporate parent is the task of creating a stable, secure and consistent environment that provides boundaries that are clear and strong enough to nurture and protect and yet permeable enough to engage the child's pre-existing relationships, particularly those that derive from his or her birth family and which maintain a view of the child's longer-term future.

EFFECTIVENESS

Findings of research into residential care in the mid and late 1980s suggested that:

> overall outcomes may be quite positive in spite of the deficiencies in the care system. (DHSS 1985, p.13)

> Short, medium and even lengthy periods in care or accommodation can be beneficial and may be the appropriate and least detrimental way to help particular children. (DOH 1991c, p.35)

Current evidence would suggest that, in the short term, as we have noted, the secondary problems associated with 'stigma, separation and strained relationships' (Bullock, Little and Milham 1993, p.16) can be formidable but that in the longer term:

> ...residential care confers educational benefits and offers children stability in an otherwise disrupted life. Certain psychological gains can also be made and useful social skills acquired. Some beneficial change may, of course, result from the maturation process. Indeed, a major contribution of residential care may simply lie in its capacity to accommodate children, thus offering them an environment for their growing up. (Bullock, Little and Milham 1993, p.17)

CONCLUSION

Residential care will continue to perform an indispensable role in looking after children. It will continue to carry out a multiplicity of functions in response to continuing changes in the population of young people whose needs it sets out to meet. Just as there are weaknesses, there are many strengths on which to build. Recent legislative initiatives, some of which we consider below, will assist in the development of a service which continues to provide a home for tens of thousands of children and young people but the current debate about the nature and the potential of residential care is a good deal more complex than is often suggested and, we would suggest, *all* social workers have a part to play in developing residential policy and practice.

 HOME FROM HOME?

We have seen how the process of separation can cause enormous difficulties and anxieties for everyone involved. There is ample research evidence (see DOH 1991c) to suggest that longer term dissolution or disruption of family links is also enormously disadvantageous to the child concerned. The preservation of family links, including sibling links, is vital to ensure 'continuity, roots and identity' (DOH 1991c, p.22), given the instability of much of the care system and in order to avoid lengthy and unnecessary extensions to the period for which a child remains in care. The concept of inclusive parental responsibility implied by the Act (see Study Texts 3.3 and 3.4) and a statutory duty to promote contact between parents and looked after children (CA 1989, sch.2, Para.15(1) see Study Text 5.3) provide a legislative impetus to preserve family links. However, translating strategic intent into practical reality is rarely straightforward. This is especially so when the policies (if not the politics) are personal, which is the case in the context of foster care.

Many of the same questions concerning role, function, organisation and effectiveness could be asked about foster care as they have been of residential care:

> Should care by the family of origin break down, will a form of foster family care be the option of first resort? If so, what objectives will the foster family seek to meet where children's rights are emphasized? How are we to articulate the relationship between the fostered child, the foster carer, and the family of origin?... Will the need be for a highly professionalised, quasi-colleague as foster carer, or are we to see a return to the traditional model as we seek to weave the magic of family care around children deprived of the experience at home? Or will...warehousing be enough? (Butler and Owens 1993, pp.40–41)

The following Exercise provides you with an opportunity to explore some of these questions further.

Exercise 5.2: Rebecca's Story

Read the following account of Rebecca's placement with foster carers and answer the questions that follow.

> The Griffith family is registered as a short-term foster carer for babies and very young children. The Griffiths' have two children of their own: Bethan aged 10 and Michael aged 6. One day a social worker telephones and asks if the family could possibly stretch to taking a 7-year-old girl, Rebecca, who has been removed from home. Her 13-year-old sister has made allegations against her father of serious sexual abuse. The social worker explains that there are no other foster homes available and that the next step is to try and find a place in a residential unit. The Griffiths agree to accept

Rebecca on a temporary basis. They know that it means making up a bed in Bethan's small bedroom but the family are confident that she will not object.

Rebecca arrives. She lives in one of the large council estates in town where there were riots a year or two ago. Rebecca is dirty, ill-clad and has nits. She has a small bag of dirty smelling clothes. She is brought in by her mother and the social worker. Mum looks dirty and bedraggled. She does not speak during her short stop at the house. Rebecca seems unperturbed by her departure.

During the next few days and weeks the Griffiths find clothes for Rebecca that Bethan has grown out of. It becomes difficult to recognise this, smart, clean and smiling Rebecca as the child who first arrived on the Griffith's doorstep. She settles well into school and is beginning to form a strong relationship with Bethan.

One major concern, however, is her father, who keeps ringing up. He appears to talk to Rebecca as if she is an adult. He cries and says that he is missing her. Rebecca is very distressed after these calls. The social worker is trying to arrange supervised contact with the father, who can be very violent. In the event, contact takes place in the residential unit where Rebecca's sister lives. The first contact session does not go well and the father accuses everyone, the Griffiths included, of stealing his daughter from him. Rebecca refuses to attend any more contact sessions. Her father is still ringing daily.

Rebecca continues to live with the Griffiths as care proceedings are begun. A social worker is visiting to talk to Rebecca about the sexual abuse. The Griffiths tell him that Rebecca is telling Bethan and Michael what happened to her and Bethan has already asked whether her daddy would ever do such a thing. The Griffiths are not involved in the counselling sessions with the social worker although they comfort Rebecca when she has dreams afterwards. The final hearing is due shortly and a case conference is to be held within a few days.

TASKS:

1. Describe what you think the appropriate relationship should be between:

    (a) Rebecca and each member of the Griffith family

    (b) Each member of the Griffith Family and members of Rebecca's birth family

    (c) The social worker and Rebecca, her birth family and the Griffiths.

2. Which of the following best describes the role of this foster carer as you understand it:

    (a) Substitute parent

    (b) Volunteer

    (c) Colleague

    (d) Employee

    (e) Client

    (f) Rival.

    Add any terms of your own that would help to describe the work that this carer undertakes. Explain your reasons.

3. What are the advantages/disadvantages of maintaining Rebecca's family links in this situation?

 **Points to Consider**

1. Has Rebecca been placed *in* or *with* the Griffith family?

2. What kind of skills or prior training would you require of foster carers working with children like Rebecca?

3. How much of a voice in decision making would/should a foster carer have in situations like this?

4. What are the differences in the kind of parenting provided by a foster carer and the kind of parenting usually provided by a child's birth family?

5.   What responsibility does the social worker have for the effects of this placement on each member of the Griffith family?

6.   What motivates people to become foster carers? Would you consider becoming one? Why/ not?

THE CORPORATE PARENT

As noted previously, the Children Act 1989 contains provisions that reflect what are known to be some of the determinants of successful outcomes for looked after children. Several of the principles on which the Act and its associated Regulations and Guidance are based reflect the obligations the corporate parent has to the looked after child:

> These obligations cover – of course – material well being and provision for appropriate education and training, health care and employment, leisure and continuing interest and support after discharge from care. They also involve helping the child develop personal skills and preferences, a sense of personal identity and worth, a sense of security and a sense of family life. (Utting 1991, p.26)

Specifically, the Act is said to recognise that (DOH 1990a):

- Admission to public care is in itself a risk to be balanced against others.

- The option of placement with family or friends should be explored before other forms of placement are considered.

- If substitute care is required, both the child and its family should be helped to make an informed choice about the most appropriate form of care.

- Every step should be taken to ensure a speedy return home if a child is provided with substitute care.

- Parents should be expected and enabled to remain involved, consistent with the welfare of the child, even if a child does need to live away from home.

- Siblings should not be separated unless the needs of the children require it.

- Family links and contact between parents and children must be actively maintained.

- The extended family matters too.

- Continuity of relationships is important and attachments should be respected, sustained and developed.

- A change of placement carries a degree of risk.

- Corporate parenting is not 'good enough' on its own. Every child and young person needs at least one individual to whom s/he is 'special', who retains responsibility over time, who is involved in plans and decisions and who has ambitions for the child's achievement and full development.

The following Study Text describes the specific provisions of the Children Act as they give effect to these principles. The requirements of the Act's associated Regulations are described in Study Text 8.2.

Study Text 5.3: The Children Act 1989 and the Looked After Child

DEFINITIONS

Children are 'looked after' when they are *either* 'in care' by virtue of a formal order made by a court *or* they are 'being provided with accommodation' through a voluntary arrangement under the Act (s.22(1)).

GENERAL DUTIES

The local authority has a duty to all the children that it looks after. This is set out at s.22(3):

(a) to safeguard and promote his welfare; and

(b) to make such use of services available for children cared for by their own parents as appears to the authority reasonable in his case.

In addition, the local authority is under a general duty towards all the children that it looks after, or is proposing to look after, to consult widely before making any decisions concerning that child. The local authority must, so far as is reasonably practicable, ascertain the wishes and feelings of:

(i)   the child

(ii) the parents

(iii) any person who has parental responsibility for the child.

(iv) any other person whose wishes and feelings the authority considers to be relevant (s.22(4)).

It must give due consideration to these wishes and feelings (s.22(5)(b)). It must also give due consideration 'to the child's religious persuasion, racial origin and cultural and linguistic background' (s.22(5)(c)). However, these duties may be overridden when it is necessary to protect members of the public from serious injury (s.22(6)).

SPECIFIC DUTIES

1. It is the duty of the local authority looking after a child to provide accommodation and maintain that child (s.23(1)).

2. The local authority must make arrangements enabling the child to live with a parent or other person connected with the child 'unless that would not be reasonably practicable or consistent with his welfare' (s.23(6)).

3. The local authority must, so far as is reasonably practicable and consistent with the child's welfare, secure that the accommodation is near the child's home and that where siblings are being accommodated, they are accommodated together (s.23(7)).

4. The local authority must appoint an independent visitor for the child where communication between the child and parents has been infrequent or where s/he has not been visited for 12 months, if it would be in the child's best interest (sch.2, para.17(1)).

5. The local authority providing accommodation for a disabled child must secure so far as is reasonably practicable that the accommodation is not unsuitable to the child's particular needs (s.23(8)).

6. The local authority is required, unless it is not reasonably practicable or consistent with the child's welfare, to endeavour to promote contact between the child and his/her parents, relatives, friends and others connected with the child (sch.2, para.15(1)).

7. The local authority must allow the child in care reasonable contact with his/her parents, guardian and any other person with whom the child was living under a residence order, or an order under the inherent jurisdiction of the High Court, immediately before the care order was made (s.34(1)).

8. The local authority is required by regulations to conduct regular reviews of the circumstances of and plans for children it is looking after (s.26).

9. The local authority must establish a procedure for considering representations (including complaints) made to it both by children it is looking after and other children in need, their parents, local authority foster-parents and other persons whom the local authority considers have a sufficient interest in the children's welfare (s.26(3)). There must be an independent person involved in the procedure (s.26(4)).

 **GOOD ENOUGH PARENTING?**

It should be noted that to support the implementation and evaluation of both the letter and the spirit of the Act, some very useful guides to practice with looked after children have been developed in recent years. Arguably, the most significant of these has been the systematised structure for assessment, planning and review developed by Professor Roy Parker and colleagues. A brief account of these is given in Study Text 7.2. Yet despite the Act, guidance, regulations, research evidence and examples of good practice, the quality of the service provided will only improve significantly if the attitudes, values and knowledge base of those directly working with looked after children are themselves subject to scrutiny and review. As the poet TS Eliot observed, there is little to be gained by dreaming of systems so perfect that no one will need to be good. The essentials of good practice in residential or foster care are the same as those of good practice anywhere. The last exercise in this Unit will give you the opportunity of reflecting on how you can apply your own standards of 'good enough' parenting and 'good enough' social work in the context of looking after children.

 Exercise 5.3: David's Story

Read the following account of David's first experience of being looked after and answer the questions that follow.

Day One – Friday Night

A telephone call from the Emergency Duty Team is received at Paddlebrook Residential Unit at 1.00 a.m. It is a request for a placement for a 15-year-old youth. He had been missing from home for a few days and upon his return his mother had been afraid to let him in. Father is out of town at the moment. Social Services were called by a neighbour after David was seen 'wandering the streets'. His mother refuses to have him home until father gets back and agrees to the social worker providing accommodation for David.

David asks the social worker to take him around to his uncle's, who lives across town, as he will look after him. The social worker refuses to do so as he says he does not have time and has made other arrangements. At 2.00 a.m. the Out of Hours social worker brings the young person in. The social worker says he was busy, hence the delay, and then leaves almost immediately. He leaves behind details of the young person's name and his address.

The 'sleeping in' residential social worker deals with the admission, much to his annoyance as he has to be on shift again in the morning. He makes his feelings very clear to the waking night staff. With David in the room, he takes the opportunity to complain about how the emergency social worker had dealt with the whole business. David is given a quick physical examination by a member of the night staff. David is told that he is just looking for bruises and any signs of infection. No toothbrush, soap or towel can be found for David, who is looking quite grubby and disheveled. A bed has to be made up and there is a problem of finding a full set of bedclothes. Eventually David is sent up to bed without supper or a drink, his clothes are taken from him, his pockets emptied and his clothes taken down to the laundry.

Day Two – Saturday Morning

David stays in bed waiting to be told he can get up. He can't find his clothes. A log entry is made that David wouldn't get up. David is given a track-suit belonging to some past resident and comes downstairs. He has missed breakfast. A social worker who had called to collect another young person, and who specialises in home finding, is told all about last night's admission. This discussion takes place in the office with all but one member of staff present. This member of staff complains about being left with the kids all morning. David sits and watches TV. At lunchtime David refuses to eat the food that is offered to him. He approaches a member of staff whom he addresses as 'Sir', much to everyone's amusement, and says he doesn't like it. He is told to 'like it or lump it'. A confrontation then ensues in which David loses his temper and swears at staff. A log entry is made for the afternoon staff to be especially vigilant as David is clearly potentially violent.

At 6.00 p.m. David 'absconds'. At about 6.30 p.m. David's father turns up at the residential unit. He says that he has only just found out where David was put last night. He asks to see his son. He is told that this can only happen with the social worker's permission and the area office will be open on Monday. He is sent on his way. At approximately 7.30 p.m. David returns to the unit in a calm frame of mind. He says he has been to see his uncle who would look after him until his father gets home. He offers to cook his own tea but permission is refused.

At 9.30 p.m. David leaves the unit again without permission. He is reported to the police at 10.30 p.m. as per the authority's guidelines. He is returned to the unit at 11.15 p.m. by the police. He has been glue sniffing with two other residents from the unit and is to be interviewed in the morning about the theft of glue from the local garage. He is argumentative and difficult and is manhandled into his room.

Day Three – Sunday Morning

David gets up and immediately informs the duty senior that a member of staff hit him last night. He is told to stop making such allegations or people will turn against him.

TASKS:

1. Using your knowledge of children's needs and rights, the requirements of the Children Act 1989 and your understanding of the principles of good practice in relation to looked after children, identify the points in this case when social workers acted inappropriately.

2. Suggest an alternative course of action at each of these points.

3. Try and explain why the professionals in this case acted in the way that they did.

 **Points to Consider**

1. What could David's parents have reasonably expected from the professionals in this case? What could the professionals reasonably have expected of David's parents?

2. What might David now expect of both the professionals involved and his parents?

3. What does this case tell you about the difficulties faced by the 'corporate parent'?

4. What does David's story tell you about the kind of 'secondary problems' that can overshadow the original reasons for being looked after?

5. What steps would you take now to recover the ground lost?

6. What will you do to prevent yourself being governed by the same kind of bureaucratic and organisational imperatives that produced such poor practice in this case?

CONCLUSION

When you see (or more likely hear) a small child's reaction to finding itself temporarily 'lost' in a supermarket or busy thoroughfare you can begin to appreciate the primal nature of the emotional response to separation. There are times when separation is necessary in the interests of the child's broader welfare or through force of circumstance and not all separations will be so traumatic. Some will come as a relief and all are mediated to some degree by age and experience. Nonetheless, the measure of the task facing those who will look after such children is reflected in the lost child's tears and protests. Making good the loss whilst building hope for the future is what looking after children means.

NOTES AND SELF-ASSESSMENT

1. Do you know where the photographs of you taken as a baby are kept?
2. Can you remember the bedroom you had as a teenager?
3. Have you been to a family wedding?
4. Do you know where each member of your immediate family lives?
5. What difference would it make to you if the answers you gave to questions 1 to 4 were actually the complete opposite of those that you did give?
6. Who have you lost?

RECOMMENDED READING

Utting, W. (1991) *Children in the Public Care – A Review of Residential Care.*
London: SSI/HMSO.
Jackson, S. and Kilroe, S. (1996) *Looking After Children: Good Parenting, Good
Outcomes – Reader.* London: HMSO.
Hoghughi, M. (1988) *Treating Problem Children – Issues, Methods and Practice.*
London: Sage.

TRAINER'S NOTES

Exercise 5.1: Separation

This can be a difficult exercise for groups and trainers will need to be
mindful of how painful memories can easily be triggered by this topic.
Participants should be given an absolute right not to share their accounts
with the larger group. The removal of WB can be role-played but this
requires a great deal of the person(s) playing WB herself. Quiet consideration of the issues raised is, in our view, a better way for participants to
explore the issues raised by this exercise.

Exercise 5.2: Rebecca's Story

The case material can easily be adapted to provide the scripts to role-play
the imminent case conference. Questions about role, task, status and power
emerge quite naturally in most simulated (and many real) case conferences.
An interesting variation can be introduced if the case conference (or a
simulated family conference) is asked to make arrangements for the
termination of Rebecca's placement. The issues around separation as well
as role and task are even more complex at this point.

Exercise 5.3: David's Story

Participants could be asked to use the material generated by the exercise as the basis of a procedure manual or good practice guide for field and residential workers. Alternatively, participants could be asked to write an information leaflet either for children and young people looked after or for their parents. A larger group, suitably divided, could be asked to do both. It is instructive to note the points of similarity and difference that inevitably emerge.

UNIT 6
Child Abuse

OBJECTIVES

In this unit you will:

- Explore child abuse from an emotional, intellectual and practice based perspective.
- Learn how child abuse is defined and classified.
- Consider appropriate responses to abuse.

CHILD ABUSE AND YOU

No qualifying or newly qualified social worker should be responsible for cases involving child abuse. The development of knowledge and skills in this area should form part of a social worker's post-qualifying experience and training. But, even though you are at an early stage in your professional development, it is important to begin preparing yourself for work in this area as soon as possible for you may find yourself confronted with child abuse much earlier in your career than you anticipate. You may already have a statutory duty to respond to allegations of abuse as part of your job or during training. Your preparation must precede your professional obligations and it is never too early to start. This Unit is intended to develop your awareness and understanding of what is meant by 'child abuse'. Many of the themes introduced in this Unit are developed in Unit 9, which explores key elements of child protection practice.

We have suggested several times already that *you, your* attitudes, *your* values and the knowledge that *you* bring to a situation are important influences on both the processes and the outcomes of social work with children and families. We begin this Unit by exploring what agenda you bring to work in the area of child abuse.

Any number of radio, television or newspaper headlines reporting an incident of child abuse or the conclusions of the latest inquiry into a child death would serve to demonstrate the significant emotional content of work in this area. Child abuse can raise powerful feelings in everyone, including the social worker. It is important to recognise the emotional impact child abuse has on you. Ignoring your emotional responses may interfere with the work you are trying to do. Once acknowledged, however, you can use your own emotional responses to practical effect. Exercise 6.1 will demonstrate what we mean.

Exercise 6.1: A Personal Account

The account below was written specifically for the purposes of this exercise by someone who had been abused as a child. Although very graphic in some ways, you will have to supply most of the details of what took place yourself.

Read the text, take a few minutes to think about it and then carry out the tasks below.

> There are two things that I remember more clearly than anything: the fact that he could be so nice sometimes and not being able to stop thinking about it. Even days afterwards I'd think about what had happened while I was doing something else, like at school. After the physical pain had gone I still used to feel it, that it had happened – not always him doing it but the feeling afterwards and the certain knowledge that it would happen again. But then it wasn't him, in my mind, it was two other people.

> I still felt bad because I knew, somehow, that it shouldn't happen and I'd try things in my head, stupid things to try and make sure it wouldn't happen again. He was always so apologetic. I'd work

out how to stay on the right side of him but, of course, I couldn't. I certainly didn't want anyone else to know, not then. You know, when you have not done your reading or your work and you hope its not you that gets asked but you know, you just know, that you will be, its like that. You think people know already, you see, but you wish that they didn't.

If someone tells you that they love you and they're sorry then you want to believe them and you hope that its all over. Maybe I should have done more to stop it. I think perhaps that I should but I didn't. I didn't know what he felt about me then and I don't think I do now, there is no excuse.

How I didn't talk about it I don't know. What would have happened if it hadn't stopped, I don't know. You can't imagine what it did to my head when I was older. I was so angry and felt such a fool. I nearly died the first time this kid asked me out.

TASKS:

1. Make a list of words to describe how you feel about what you have read.

2. Write down how you feel about the child concerned.

3. Write down how you feel about the adult involved.

4. Write down how you feel the child and the adult may have felt at the time of the abuse and now.

 **Points to Consider**

1. Were you surprised by any of the feelings that the piece raised in you?

2. Which of the feelings that you had towards the child might be helpful to you from this point?

3. Which of the feelings that you had towards the child might be unhelpful to you from this point? For example, do you see how a feeling of anger may motivate you to work hard for this child? Do you see how anger might also cloud your judgement and make it

more likely that you will make mistakes? Do you see how fear might prompt a 'fight or flight' response?

4. What might be the consequences for you of denying those feelings that you have described?

5. What might be the consequences of showing or hiding your feelings from the child and/or the adult involved?

6. What reasons might there be for someone not wishing to acknowledge their emotional response to child abuse?

 ## INTELLECTUAL RESPONSES TO CHILD ABUSE

Whilst our initial response to an incident or account of child abuse might be at an emotional level, social workers cannot confine themselves to a response at this level only. You are required to explore intellectually what is meant by the term. You might view such a suggestion as unnecessary. Surely everyone knows what abuse is? At the extremes we might concede that there is likely to be a fairly ready consensus as to what constitutes abuse. The deliberate starving to death of a child is clearly abusive, we might assume, but in what sense is the 'quiet catastrophe' that we referred to in Unit 1 that results in 40,000 children in the developing world dying every day from malnutrition and preventable diseases abusive? Is it abusive that 100 million 6 to 11-year-olds have no school to go to (UNICEF 1991)? Risking children's health in dangerous working conditions is clearly abusive, but have you thought about where your morning coffee comes from in those terms? We do not expect you, as social workers, to take on such geo-political issues. Our point is that what we describe as abusive, even at the extremes, is selective. At the more immediate level of the kind of abuse that confronts social workers in the UK we believe there remains an essential ambiguity. Exercise 6.2 will demonstrate what we mean.

Exercise 6.2: Is it/Isn't it Abusive?

Read the following mini case studies and answer the question: 'Is or isn't it abusive?'

1. Wayne is six years old. He has some behavioural problems and is generally boisterous and disobedient. He threw a stone, narrowly missing his baby brother, and broke a downstairs window. His father made him pick up the glass. Wayne cut his hands but his father made him clear the whole room nonetheless 'as a lesson to him'.

2. John is 13. His father has a large collection of pornographic videos that he, John and several of John's school friends watch together. Most sessions include masturbation. John's father has said that he is only making sure that the boys understand the facts of life properly and that there is nothing to be ashamed of in being so 'open' about sex.

3. Julie is 14 and has run away from a children's home. She is staying with a much older man who has provided her with a home, food and clothing, but she is expected to pay for her keep by sleeping with him and working as a prostitute. Julie says that she likes the life and the money and does not want to return to care.

4. Sandra has moderate learning difficulties. She has twin boys aged 11 months. She keeps several dogs and the house is very dirty and disorganised. Sandra goes out every Thursday night and leaves the twins with the 12-year-old boy from next door. Both twins are dirty and have severe urine burns and a nappy rash. Both are underweight. Sandra says that she cannot afford to buy more nappies than she does and, as she does not have a washing machine, she cannot keep up with the twins.

5. Tom is 16. He is not very 'sporty' and prefers to spend more time with his books and computer than he does with young people his own age. He is very shy in the company of girls. Some of his classmates have begun calling him names. They say that he is 'gay'. Tom has begun to pretend to be ill in order to avoid going to

school. He says that the name calling is 'getting to him' and fears that, sooner rather than later, 'someone will sort him out' at school.

6. Rosie is 16. Her parents are devoutly religious and members of a strict religious sect. Rosie is made to dress very plainly and is not allowed cosmetics, music or to watch TV. She is not allowed out alone other than to walk to school. Her parents searched her school bag and found a 'love letter' from a classmate. Rosie was locked in her bedroom and kept away from school for over a month.

7. Megan is 13. She lives with her mother and stepfather and her two half-brothers. The boys receive almost all of their parents' attention. Megan is not included in family outings and is made to do a disproportionate amount of helping out with the household chores. She is often not allowed to eat with the rest of the family. She is constantly told that she is 'useless' and will never make anything of her life.

8. Alun and Mary live in a particularly run down and deprived area. Their prospects of work, beyond a government scheme, are practically nil. Both are very depressed at the prospect of a life on the dole and say that the only pleasure they get from life is from sex with each other and occasional solvent abuse. Both sets of parents allow them to sleep together. Both are 14. Alun's father is worried about the solvents but feels he has nothing better to offer his son.

 **Points to Consider**

1. When making your decisions, were you influenced by the nature and degree of any harm done and the degree of responsibility of the adults involved?

2. Were you influenced by the immediate or by the longer term consequences of the possible abuse?

3. Were you influenced by how much control the adult had over the circumstances in which the alleged abuse took place?

4. To what extent did the 'maturity' of the young people involved affect your decision?

5. Would the determination of abuse be different if you were to ask the children concerned? Or the adults?

6. Are you aware of anything in your own experience of childhood that might prevent you from recognising abuse?

DEFINING CHILD ABUSE

Some definitions of child abuse are provided later in this Unit. Defining abuse is not the same as explaining it, of course, and we address some of the issues that arise when trying to define abuse in Study Text 6.1.

Study Text 6.1: Defining Child Abuse

In a report, written by the Directors of Social Work in Scotland, concerning child abuse and child protection, the following honest and sobering observation is made: 'Practitioners...are working within a field of evolving knowledge and changing public attitudes and expectations. Often they find themselves at the forefront of discovery without the support of established theory' (1992, p.5).

This statement provides a number of clues as to why it is so very difficult to make unequivocal statements about child abuse, its nature, causes and appropriate responses. It is not that child abuse is a new phenomenon, rather it is that our knowledge and understanding of it are constantly evolving. Moreover, the statement hints at the fact that child abuse is a negotiated process – that is to say that both the term and the idea mean different things to different people at different times. Consequently, there remains at the very heart of our understanding of child abuse a fundamental and unavoidable uncertainty. This study text explores that uncertainty so that you can build it into your own understanding of child abuse and so that you develop an appropriate critical approach to your wider reading in this area.

We have already explored in Unit 1 how childhood is socially constructed and re-constructed, mostly by adults and often for reasons that have little to do with the rights, needs or interests of children. It is increasingly recognised that the same is true of child abuse (and child protection). There are few absolutes as, culturally and temporally, childhood is continuously defined and re-defined. Similarly, child abuse and child protection services cannot be understood without reference to the way in which we account for, and respond to, children generally.

It is perfectly possible, for example, to trace an explanatory, therapeutic and analytical history of child abuse and child protection, just as it is possible to trace the social history of children. Arbitrarily, one might begin with the nineteenth-century concern with what has been called a 'narrative of the body' (Hendrick 1994) where the visible poverty, palpable squalor, physical illness and the depredations of harsh working conditions were to be remedied with cleanliness, godliness and the cottage home; through to the development of a 'narrative of the mind' where the psychic traumas of childhood are internal, individual and, latterly, sexual. History is not a linear process, however, and ideas from one period may last well into successive ages and, sometimes, of course, old lessons have to be re-learned. Nonetheless, it is simply not possible to extract the concept of abuse from the context in which it occurs and the climate of ideas in which it is defined.

Contemporary constructions of childhood rest on assumptions, as we have suggested in Unit 1, that childhood is not simply quantitatively and qualitatively different from adulthood (which is simply to state the obvious) but that children are also, *by their very nature*, inferior. This imputed inferiority refers not only to children's intellectual, emotional and cognitive capacities but also to their status as social beings and actors in their own biographies. It is not simply a matter of relative competence. It is in the cultural presumption of the inferior social status of childhood that we locate their consequent powerlessness and it is this relative powerlessness that is implicated in any explanation of the phenomenon of abuse itself. Unsurprisingly, such a construction of childhood has had profound effects on the process and structures of child protective services in the UK. If children are generally, and almost by definition, viewed as incompetent and inferior, yet fully understood by adults, it is no surprise that some children are abused nor is it a surprise that child protection measures may prove incapable of adequately protecting some children.

Growing awareness of this has led to the development, in recent years, of 'ecological' accounts that locate abuse in the various power relationships in society and which argue for responses to child abuse that are more broadly preventative and which emphasise children's rights. Such approaches can be criticised on the grounds that they may absolve individual abusers of responsibility and that there is a fine line between respecting a child's rights and leaving them to fend for themselves.

Clearly, *any* explanation, categorisation or definition of child abuse carries the impression of the precise moment in which it is made and conveys as much about those making the distinctions as it does about the phenomenon itself. Consider how child abuse might be defined (and explained) depending on where one stood in relation to the events in question. Here we are not referring to any particular incident of abuse but to the idea of child abuse itself.

We might identify several 'stakeholders' in any account of child abuse: first, the community at large have a legitimate interest in that the public 'wants children protected from a variety of depredations: it wants parents' rights and family life to be safeguarded against unwarranted interference by the State;…and it expects all of this to be done quietly, smoothly, efficiently and effectively' (Parker *et al.* 1991, p.20). Second, practitioners, based on their training and experience, will have particular views on what constitutes abuse. This may owe more to their sense of what can be done to manage a particular set of circumstances than any particular theoretical orientation, of course. Third, resource gatekeepers, elected members and management committees may also have an interest in defining abuse in terms of their own strategic interests and responsibilities. If resources are limited, eligibility thresholds can shift. Fourth, the families of vulnerable children are clearly actual and potential contributors to how abuse is defined. Then there is the child him or herself.

Hitherto, the child's account of abuse has had very little impact on how the phenomenon is understood and acted upon by adults (Butler 1996b). Bullying, for example, would almost certainly rate much more highly on children's hierarchy of abuse than it does on adults'. Bullying may actually result in the death of more children than any other form of 'abuse'.

We have hinted already that certain forms of harm or injury to certain categories of children would not constitute abuse for many adults (e.g. racism in this country or starvation amongst children living in the developing world; bullying and corporal punishment in the UK or child labour and economic exploitation elsewhere; certain categories of asylum seekers in the UK or refugees in 'foreign' wars). Depending on your point of view, and relationship to the events in question, your definitions of, and explanations for, abuse may be different from ours. What matters, however, is that in your reading around these issues, that will extend well beyond the confines of this particular book, you examine critically, carefully and comprehensively any definition, explanation or account that you encounter. Certainly not all, maybe not any, definitions of abuse are wholly reliable, valid or exhaustive.

A fundamental uncertainty around what constitutes abuse is at the heart of work in this field. It finds a significant echo in direct work too. Living with the uncertainty, rather than ignoring it or taking refuge in simple (and simplistic) explanations or definitions, is one of the most difficult steps in developing as an effective professional capable of working in this field. At the heart of good child protection social work lies the exercise of good judgement. The next exercise reinforces the point.

Exercise 6.3: Defining Abuse

Below you will find six thumbnail 'definitions' of abuse. Read them carefully and jot down, for each one, an example of what is being described. Then go back and read the mini case descriptions provided for Exercise 6.2 before completing the tasks set out below.

1. *Physical Abuse*: where a parent (or somebody else caring for a child) physically hurts, injures or kills a child.
2. *Sexual Abuse*: when adults seek sexual gratification by using children.
3. *Neglect*: where parents (or whoever else is caring for the child) fail to meet the basic essential needs of children (e.g. adequate food, clothes, warmth and health care).

4. *Emotional Abuse*: where children are harmed by constant lack of love and affection, or threats.

5. *Deprivation*: where children's needs fail to be met or their potential and life-chances are damaged by social forces and/or institutions.

6. *Exploitation*: where individuals and social institutions (including institutions of the State) satisfy their own needs or purposes by inappropriately using children.

TASKS:

1. Allocate each of the mini case descriptions to one or more categories of abuse.

2. Describe clearly your reasons for doing so.

3. Describe how adequate each definition is for each case.

4. Amend each of the thumbnail definitions to reflect your appreciation of the cases and your broader understanding of abuse.

   And/Or

5. Rank order the cases – first from the point of view of the child concerned and then from the (imagined) point of view of the editor of the local tabloid newspaper.

 **Points to Consider**

1. Was it difficult to place particular cases in single categories?

2. What does this tell you about the phenomenon and the concept of abuse?

3. Whose definition of abuse counts for the most and why?

4. Whose definition of abuse counts the least and why?

5. How adequate is your own definition of abuse?

6. What are you going to do to improve it?

RESPONDING TO ABUSE

As someone who wants to work with children and families, part of your motivation, we assume, is that you want to do something to stop or reduce child abuse. We have seen how difficult it can be to determine what abuse means. Not surprisingly, it is equally difficult to work out in practice what protecting a child involves exactly. Sometimes, for example, the removal of a child from his or her home may be protective. Sometimes such a separation will prove harmful (see Unit 5). At this stage in your professional development, you may not be in a position to make such judgements. That does not mean, however, that you have no obligation to respond to situations in which child abuse may have taken place. The final part of this unit deals with responding to child abuse, when you are least prepared for it and least expecting it.

Not everyone confronted with a potential incidence of abuse will respond. Unless the abuse is very obvious (and it rarely is) it may be possible to persuade yourself that you don't have 'enough evidence' on which to act. You may persuade yourself that the child is 'making it up' or 'attention seeking'. You may not want to find yourself caught up in an investigation or a court appearance at a later date. The incident may reawaken bad memories of your own. All of these reasons for not responding are understandable but ultimately insufficient, especially if you consider the consequences of inaction if your suspicions are well founded.

If the abuse is not stopped it is impossible for a child to receive the help they may need to redress the damage they have experienced. If abuse takes place and the abuser is not prevented from re-abusing it may be that other children may also be in danger. These are powerful reasons why we should all take our responsibilities very seriously if we suspect that abuse is happening.

So what should you do? Exercise 6.4 examines how you might react if a child was to disclose abuse to you.

Exercise 6.4: Jane's Story

Read the following case scenario and answer the questions. Complete each individual section before attempting the next.

> Jo, a student social worker, is taking her daughter to Brownies and the Leader asks to have a word with her. She starts by apologising and says that she knows that Jo is something to do with Social Services. 'Can I talk to you in confidence?' She asks, 'It's about Jane. I'm very worried about the bruises she has on her face and arms'.

1. What would your response be to a request for confidentiality in a situation such as this?

> Jo has a look and is appalled at what she sees. Jo asks Jane how she got the bruises.

2. Was this the right thing to do in the circumstances? If not, what else could Jo have done?

> Jane starts to cry and says that she fell over. She begs Jo not to say anything to anyone else. She seems really upset. Jo is beginning to feel a bit embarrassed about all the fuss and wishes that she had not become involved in the first place. Jane is clearly relieved when Jo tells her not to worry, Jo is not going to say anything.

3. a) Is this how you might have reacted?

    b) What are the possible consequences of Jo's decision not to tell a child protection worker.

> Later that night Jo realises that the incident with Jane is bothering her. It gives her a restless night. The next day Jo mentions it to a colleague who says that Jo ought to discuss it with someone from the child care team. Jo delays doing this all day and finally, at 4.45pm, she goes and talks to the child care team senior.

4. What are the consequences of this delay:

    (a) if Jane's injuries were sustained from an assault?

    (b) if Jane really had simply fallen down the stairs?

The team senior listens to Jo's description of the bruises and is very interested in the fact that Jane was distressed and begged Jo not to tell anyone else. The team leader decides that there is sufficient reason to investigate further.

5. What are the possible consequences now if:

    (a) Jane has been abused?

    (b) Jane has not been abused?

6. Could Jo have done anything else which might have assisted the investigation which will now take place?

Compare your answers with those given in the Trainer's Notes for this Unit, which are based on Study Text 6.3.

Points to Consider

1. List some possible reasons for someone in Jo's position not wishing to 'get involved'. Might any of these apply to you?

2. What might Jane be expecting from someone to whom she does tell her story?

3. What particular needs of the child should your response be directed towards meeting?

4. What particular rights of the child must your response respect?

5. Are there any circumstances in which you would break your promise of confidentiality once given?

6. What does your answer to Question 5 tell you about your personal construction of childhood?

Study Text 6.2: Responding to Abuse

Unit 9 deals in more detail with the process of investigation following an allegation or suspicion of abuse. The purpose of this Study Text is to help to prepare you for exposure to abuse when investigation is not explicitly part of your professional role. It is presented in the form of five 'bullet points' in the hope that you will be able to easily absorb and recall what is required of you.

- Listen: if someone, particularly the child directly concerned, begins to tell you about a possible abusive incident or series of events, listen. Do not 'cross-examine' the child or begin some form of quasi-investigation.

- Be supportive: it is important that the child feels supported and that you do not transmit any of the anxieties that you may have to the child. In the exercise above, this support could have been offered by the social worker or by the Brownie Leader with the social worker's support. Jane may have found it easier to talk to the Brownie leader, whom she knows better. You will need to balance any emotional response that you may have with an appropriate intellectual response.

- Don't judge: it is vital that you do not patronise the child or otherwise seek to diminish what you are being told. Keep the information that you are being given separate from your interpretation of it. It may prove necessary to repeat what the child says to the child protection workers later and it may be helpful to make notes of what you have been told, as soon as practicable, after you have spoken to the child.

- Don't make promises that you can't keep: particularly, do not promise a child unconditional confidentiality unless you are prepared to maintain it, no matter what you are subsequently told. Be honest. It is far preferable to say to anyone, child or adult, who asks you not to tell: 'I don't know what you are going to tell me. I may have to talk to someone-else but, if I can keep what you tell me in confidence, I will'.

- Don't dither: check out your concerns with a more experienced worker and report them to a senior worker in your agency, ideally your line manager. Delay, in Jane's case for example, could have led to the bruises, that is the 'proof', fading and the opportunity for her to be further harmed. Or, if she hadn't been assaulted, delay may have made it more difficult for her parents to convince the social worker that the faded bruises were the result of a fall.

 **CONCLUSION**

We have suggested in this Unit that a central element in working in this field is an acknowledgement of the essential uncertainty and ambiguity that surrounds child abuse. There are no simple check-lists that you can apply to determine whether abuse is taking place or not; there are no simple steps you can take to make the abuse go away or magically 'get better'. You will go on to learn how to understand, evaluate and reduce the risks for the child and the worker in child protection situations as your career develops but you may find yourself involved long before you think you are fully ready. At this point in your professional development we would want you to think carefully about what you see or are told about child abuse and to critically evaluate and reflect on your wider reading.

But, most importantly of all, we want you to be ready to act when your suspicions are aroused. There can be no justification for simply turning away.

NOTES AND SELF-ASSESSMENT

1. Are there certain forms of behaviour that you would always categorise as abusive?

2. How does your understanding of abuse relate to your particular construction of childhood?

3. What are the major influences on your understanding of abuse?

4. Do all instances of child abuse require action?

5. What might stop you from responding to any abuse of which you become aware?

6. Do you know *how* to take the appropriate next step in responding to abuse in your particular post or practice placement?

RECOMMENDED READING

Rogers, W.S., Hevey, D. and Ash, E. (1992) (eds) *Child Abuse and Neglect – Facing the Challenge*. Milton Keynes: OUP.

Stevenson, O. (1989) (ed) *Child Abuse: Professional Practice and Public Policy*. London: Harvester Wheatsheaf.

Cloke, C. and Davies, M. (1995) *Participation and Empowerment in Child Protection*. London: Pitman.

TRAINER'S NOTES

Exercise 6.1: A Personal Account

Encourage group members to share feelings, possibly by 'quickthinking' them on to a flip chart. You may wish to consider the range of feelings expressed and their intensity. Are there feelings that are commonly felt? Are some much more personal than others? (Group members should be reminded that they do not have to explain or 'justify' their responses). One important aspect to consider is whether some of the feelings expressed would be helpful in working with a family where abuse was suspected. If so, to whom would they be helpful? In the exercise, for example, we note how anger can be both a negative and positive influence – negative in the sense of rendering a worker unable to hear the needs of the person who has been abused, positive in the sense of providing the energy to 'do' something in the face of other overbearing emotions. What other feelings amongst those you have elicited from the group might have similar double-edged effects?

Exercise 6.2: Is it/Isn't it Abusive

A larger group could be broken down into pairs and the decisions compared and debated between sub-groups. A much more effective (but much more difficult to manage) way to proceed is to work in a large group and to take each case in turn and to proceed only when unanimous agreement has been reached. This has the advantage of making participants explore in fine detail their reasons for whatever view they hold and it makes visible the kind of disagreements that really do exist about the nature of various forms of abuse.

Exercise 6.3: Defining Abuse

This exercise can be used in a group in the same way as for the preceding exercise. For Task 4, sub-groups or pairs can work together to produce definitions that can be debated and 'adopted' by the whole group. Task 5 is best done by two 'opposing' groups, who complete their rankings and then, in role, argue the merits of their case.

Exercise 6.4: Jane's Story

The case material can either:

(a) be given to each student as it is and the whole group works individually on the answers,

or

(b) be read out by the trainer, posing the questions in sequence and having group discussion,

or

(c) be prepared as a booklet for use in small groups. The booklets would have a scenario and question on each page so that issues could be discussed before the next instalment was revealed on the following page.

The following are some suggestions for discussion 'prompts':

1. What would your response be to a request for confidentiality in a situation such as this?

   • You can't guarantee confidentiality

   • It's difficult to say no.

2. Was this the right thing to do in the circumstances? If not, what else could Jo have done?

   • Depends on how it is done. Might be OK if Jo is subtle but perhaps a bit overpowering for Jane who, after all, doesn't know Jo.

   • Perhaps better to talk only with the Leader and enable her to do the talking to Jane and pass on information to Jo.

3. Is this how you might have reacted? After all, the bruises could have been caused by a fall.

   • Has Jo the right to tell Jane that she will respect her confidence and not tell anyone else?

   • What do you think Jane might be feeling now?

   • How swayed are you by Jane's distress?

   • What are the possible consequences of a decision not to tell a child protection worker?

   • Consequences: Jane might be more severely bruised tomorrow.

- Jane might be terrified to tell anyone again.

4. What are the consequences of this delay:

   (a) if Jane's injuries were sustained from an assault:

   - Bruises will fade and 'proof' of harm will be more difficult to come by.

   - More opportunities for Jane to be further harmed.

   (b) if Jane had really simply fallen down the stairs:

   - Nothing for Jane but if the SSD decide, when they are informed, that there is a case to investigate the fact that there are faded bruises might make it more difficult for Jane's carers to convince the social worker that it was simply a case of a fall.

5. What are the possible consequences now if:

   (a) Jane has been abused:

   - Jane may be protected from further abuse.

   - The perpetrator may be stopped from harming Jane or any other children in the household.

   - Jane will be given the opportunity to talk about what has happened to her, to let out some of her distress. This may be the start of action to repair any damage, mental or physical.

   - The family will experience disruption and investigation by outsiders.

   (b) Jane has not been abused.

   - The family, of which Jane is a part, will experience disruption and stress.

   - Jane herself may feel guilty for setting the investigation in progress.

   - If Jane feels that she is not believed then the protection may seem more like persecution.

6. Could Jo have done anything else which might have assisted the enquiry?

- Enabled Brownie Leader to collect together clear information about what she had seen.

- Written down what she had seen; time, extent, reasons given, Jane's comments, etc.

- Told the Brownie Leader who to contact and offer to go with her.

- Been more honest with Jane and explained that she is very concerned about her bruises and the fact that she seems very frightened.

PART II
Developing Specialist Knowledge and Skills

UNIT 7

Assessing

OBJECTIVES

In this unit you will:

- Explore the context in which assessments are made.

- Learn some practical techniques for gathering and ordering information.

- Critically review contemporary frameworks for assessment in child care.

- Begin work on an extended case study and consider the application of what you have learned to practice.

 **IN THE BEGINNING**

'In any social work situation, you should always start at the beginning.' That sounds like the kind of common-sense advice that you might expect to find in a book like this. The trouble is that the 'beginning' can be a very difficult place to find! Even if you are the first point of contact for people using the services of your particular agency, the situation that prompted the referral will obviously have a history that extends beyond your introduction into events. All of the individuals, families or groups involved will also have histories, both discrete and interconnected. It might be more appropriate, although not very helpful, to seek 'the beginning' in the 'life, universe and everything' kind of question that we usually associate with philosophers or theologians. The truth is that your involvement in any child and family situation never occurs 'at the beginning'. You are always going to be joining in a sequence of events that is already in progress and which will continue long after your involvement has ended.

We make this very obvious point for two reasons: first, because some social workers and other professionals can forget that this is the case and assume that nothing of importance or interest could conceivably have pre-dated their arrival on the scene and, second, because, uncluttered by too many facts, it is all too easy to go on to make judgements about the problem and how it is to be tackled. These assumptions have much more to do with what the worker brings to the situation than with what the family brings and are usually unproductive, if not actually harmful.

The key to avoiding them lies in a commitment to the process of assessment. The reference to 'commitment' is deliberate. It is perfectly possible to proceed to action without assessing the circumstances or context in which that action takes place, with potentially disastrous results. We can all be too busy, too stressed or too confident in our diagnostic skills. We refer to a '*process* of assessment' deliberately too. Assessment isn't an event. It is not something you do once to someone else and exclusively for your own purposes. Assessment is a continuous and mutual process of making sense of what has happened and what is happening now.

Veronica Coulshed offers a very useful definition of assessment which she describes as a 'perceptual/analytic process of selecting, categorising, organising and synthesising data' (1988, p.13) with the main purpose of assessment being to develop an 'informed impression leading to action' (Timms and Timms 1982, p.16). The process of assessment 'leads the worker and the client to a better understanding of the reasons or causes for the problem and the factors that may aid or hinder its resolution.' (Cournoyer 1991, p.8).

The purpose of this Unit is to encourage you to critically reflect on the various models of assessment that you might encounter or use in practice and to introduce to you some common, practical and easily adapted techniques that might assist you in any assessment in which you might become involved.

So, even if we can't really start at the beginning, where can we begin the assessment?

If assessment is to be understood in broad terms as making sense of what has happened and what is happening now, the obvious place to start is with the information that you have in front of you. Often the most immediate and voluminous, if not necessarily the most accessible, source of information will be in the form of a case file. Such files come in all sorts of shapes, sizes, colours and degrees of organisation. As a student or a newly qualified worker, perhaps the majority of your work will be encountered, in the first instance, via the case file.

As well as offering the foundation of a thorough assessment, a good working knowledge of the file has other benefits too. For example, acquaintance with the contents of the file should reduce the possibility that information previously provided to your agency will need to be repeated. Sometimes this information will have been gained at considerable cost. Your ignorance of key events already known to your agency will convey an unhelpful sense that what has been shared previously has been forgotten or discounted. You will have more time available for the task in hand if you do not have to trawl for information that your agency already possesses. Moreover, confidence in you and your ability to help will inevitably be diminished if you make a point of demonstrating that you have not had either the time or the inclination to prepare adequately. The following Study Text demonstrates some ways in which you might begin the process of assessment by exploring how you can make most use of such a file.

Study Text 7.1: Starting Points

One key dimension along which we ordinarily fix and structure our own experience is by reference to time. Many interventive techniques, particularly those derived from the psychoanalytic tradition of casework, rely on establishing a detailed and accurate chronology of events as a basis for interpreting and understanding current situations and motivations. Even if you do not intend to base your own practice in this tradition, establishing the order of events is a useful first step towards developing your understanding of the events and processes in which you are becoming involved.

Most case files are, nominally at least, compiled in chronological order. However, whilst case notes may be sequential, they often cross-refer to other sections of the file – such as correspondence or reports which may be ordered thematically or in relation to particular events. In reality, the 'time-lines' can be very difficult to trace through even a relatively recent file. You could begin to get a sense of past events simply by writing the year down on one side of a piece of paper and, using the file, writing down the significant events of that year alongside. Alternatively, you could use a card index record – this allows you a little more flexibility to add additional information as your assessment proceeds. You could also represent the information graphically, in the form of a flow chart. With a little imagination, the flow chart could be turned into a river or a railway line that might help to elicit further information later in the assessment or to interpret the flow of events to a younger child as part of your direct work with them.

A second key dimension along which we fix and order our experience is by reference to patterns of relationships. The nature of relationships can also be a focus for specific interventions and is usually an important consideration in child and family work. One commonly used technique for representing relationships through time is the genogram. At its simplest, a genogram is little more than an annotated family tree. The annotations can include major family events, occupations, places of residence and even patterns of contact. The genogram uses conventional notation: a square represents a male; a circle represents a female; a triangle represents those circumstances where the sex is unknown (e.g. an unborn child or a distant relative) and a cross drawn through one of these figures represents a death. The strength of relationships between individuals are shown by lines: an enduring relationship by a firm line and a transitory relationship by a broken line. These lines can be crossed through by a single line in the event of separation or by a double line in the event of a divorce. When drawing a genogram, the children of a particular couple are usually entered according to age, starting with the oldest on the left. It can be useful to draw a dotted line around all of those living in the same household. The following example illustrates the basic form of a genogram covering three generations.

1971	1972	1973	1975	1978	1982
September 12th Born Northtown. Twins! Me 5lbs 4oz. Jane 5lbs	Whooping cough. In hospital for two weeks. Jane also poorly	Family moved house. Brother Matthew born, June 24th	Started school. Liked it. So did Jane. Started speech therapy, hated that.	March, fell off bike. Broke my arm.	Started Grammar School. Jane went to girl's school. Mum and Dad split up.

1987	1989	1990	1991	1992	1994
Took GCSE's. Did well. Jane didn't. She was very disappointed	Took 'A' levels. Got into University. Jane didn't. she started nurse training but dropped out after a few months	Dropped out of University. Joined the army.	Gulf war. Jane got married. Missed the wedding. Home on leave in September when I met Becky	February! Married Becky. Posted to Germany. Jane had baby son. Quite a year!	Back in UK. Infertility treatment started. Jane now has three children!

1995	1996	Future
Confirmation that we can't ever have children of our own. Mum dies.	Make first contact with adoption agency. Social worker starts to visit	We want to have a family of our own....

Figure 7.1 The flow chart

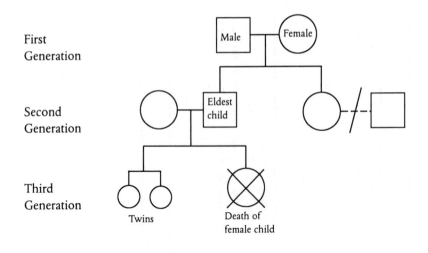

First
Generation

Second
Generation

Third
Generation

Figure 7.2 The genogram

At its best, the genogram can present very complex family relationships in a very concise and accessible form. It can highlight themes and patterns that are echoed across the generations and it can serve to map key relationships and patterns of communication.

Whilst the family is one important context in which to establish relationships, it does not always provide a big enough picture. Individuals and families have relationships with individuals and groups around them and their particular household. Such groups, or 'systems', can include neighbours, school, friends, health services, etc. One way of representing the various affiliations and the nature of a family or individual's relationships to the wider community is the ecomap. Ecomaps can be drawn for families or individuals. In either case, the key person(s) is represented by a circle in the middle of the page. Around this, sometimes at distances intended to represent the 'proximity' of the relationship, other circles are drawn that represent important connections, either to other members of the family, particular individuals or groups. As with the genogram, the lines used to join the various circles can also carry additional information: a solid line can represent a strong relationship, a dotted line a weak one and a hatched line a stressful one. Arrow heads can be added at either or both ends of the line to demonstrate the 'flow' of information, interest or resources between the parties.

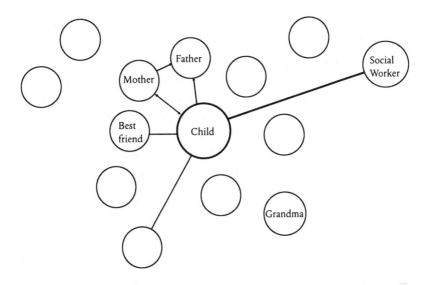

Figure 7.3 The ecomap

Whilst we have presented each of these techniques as a useful means of sorting existing information, it should be clear also how they might be used in direct work, either to elicit further information on the basis of the gaps that show up in available data or to convey or interpret information that is not shared or understood by members of the family or individuals with whom you are working.

There are some obvious dangers in the process we have described so far, however. Files can be substantially inaccurate. They can be incomplete, outdated or record as factual what is merely conjecture. Frequently, simple mistakes, such as the failure to record a date of birth accurately, can be repeated over many years. Thorough review should help identify gross errors but you should always confirm key information before acting upon it. This is an important route into the mutuality of assessment that we mentioned earlier. Sharing, comparing and reviewing the information that is the basis of your assessment is a vital part of the process of becoming engaged with the family with whom you are going to work.

In the same way that information cannot simply be taken at face value, Sheila McDonald (1991, p.49) has reminded us that the basis on which we evaluate information is far from neutral: 'On a practice level, social workers should be clear about their attitudes to the families living in our area, including their beliefs about the validity of those families' lifestyle.

This agenda which we all carry around with us, defines every piece of work undertaken with children.'

The essentially subjective nature of any assessment needs to be acknowledged, even where that assessment begins conventionally enough with the 'facts on file'. Cournoyer (1991) makes the point well in his account of the several stages involved in preparing to begin direct work. He describes what we have encouraged you to do so far as 'preparatory reviewing' and goes on to explore 'preparatory empathy' and 'preparatory self-exploration'. Preparatory empathy involves the worker imaginatively recreating the salient issues from the service user's point of view. This may heighten your sensitivity to the thoughts and feelings that others may have about the 'facts' of their life. Preparatory self-exploration is intended to identify the potential negative impact on the service user of the worker's characteristics, biases, emotional tender spots, 'unfinished business' and prejudices. It is also a very specific way of making explicit your commitment to anti-oppressive practice. Both preparatory empathy and preparatory self-exploration, however tentative, will demonstrate to you how much assessment is more of an interpretative art rather than an exact science and, as such, has always carried the indelible signature of its makers.

 **A CASE IN POINT**

If you are fortunate, many of the files that will be allocated to you will contain a summary prepared when the case was last closed or in anticipation of its transfer. What follows is a representation of such a summary, with the addition of a report of the most recent events that have led to the particular family involved presenting themselves at the Southtown Social Services Department. Assume that you are working in a child and family team in the Social Services Department and that the case is being allocated to you. Read through the file and then attempt the exercise that follows.

Taylor Family Case File
BACKGROUND INFORMATION

Alison (1/3/89) and Michael (5/6/90) live with their mother, Tracy (2/2/73). Tracy prefers to be known as Tracy Taylor, her family name, since her divorce from Ron Jones, Alison and Michael's father, in June 96. No formal court orders concerning the children were made during the divorce.

Ron now lives in Northtown, some 140 miles away. He remarried 18 months ago. He has a new-born son, Wayne. Ron is an electrician by trade and it is believed that he has begun to build up a successful business with his cousin in Northtown. Tracy has had another child since the divorce, John (1/12/97). His father, Alun Evans, lives with Tracy and the three children at her council-owned house in New Estate, Southtown.

Alun and Tracy have been living together for three years. No record exists of previous contact with Alun. Previous social workers do not seem to have seen him at all, although there is a note saying that Mr Evans would not meet the social worker as he had 'had enough of them when he was a kid'.

Tracy and Ron met when she was still at school. She became pregnant before she left and married Ron, four years her senior, just days after her sixteenth birthday. Her family has been known to the social services department for many years. She is one of six children, the eldest four of which, including Tracy, were the subject of three-year matrimonial care orders following the breakdown of her own parents' marriage in the summer of 79. Tracy and her three older brothers and sisters were fostered briefly in 80 as there was concern for the poor standard of care the children received from Mrs. Taylor and their poor school attendance. The files relating to this period of Tracy's life have been lost and no further details are available.

When Alison was born Tracy found it very difficult to cope and moved away from her recently allocated council house in Old Estate, Southtown back to her mother's house, a few streets away. Ron went to stay with his parents in Northtown during this time (June–December 89), although he did make very frequent visits to Tracy and Alison. Mrs. Taylor (senior) still lives in Old Estate. Tracy's father died in August 90.

In November 89 there were several anonymous telephone calls stating that the child living at Mrs. Taylor's (senior) house was being neglected and that the house was in a filthy state. Two duty social workers visited and found the physical condition of the house appalling – the kitchen unhygienic, scarcely any food in the house, evidence of a recent fire in one of the bedrooms, a blocked toilet, broken glass all over the garden and dirty nappies spilling out of the bin.

Alison was clearly not well and, with Tracy's agreement, was admitted to hospital for a week. Ron visited regularly and Tracy stayed with Alison in hospital. At a child abuse case conference called before Alison was discharged from hospital it was decided, by consent, that Alison would be placed with foster carers while Ron and Tracy moved back into their former house in Old Estate. A support programme involving a family aide and regular visits from the social worker was initiated and the child was not placed on the 'at risk' register. Within a month Alison was home and, with the right kind of support and practical assistance, the family settled down and social work attention eased off gradually.

The social worker was still visiting when Michael was born. This time Tracy and Ron were better prepared and, although Tracy did not have an easy time during the later stages of pregnancy and during labour (Michael was a high forceps delivery), the early weeks at home seemed to go very well. However, in the late summer of 90 the Health Visitor reported that Tracy was becoming very depressed and was unable to look after the children properly. Ron was not always around as he was working with his cousin in Northtown and the Health Visitor was becoming concerned for the children. In her opinion, Alison was developmentally delayed and Michael was not thriving as he should. Additional support, including help from staff at the local family centre, was put in place.

The situation did seem to be holding together but Ron was clearly very distressed by all that was going on. He decided that Tracy and the children should go with him to Northtown where his family would look after them and he could see them every day. He agreed to allow a social worker from Northtown Social Services Department to call in to see that all was well.

From September 90 until October 92 the children lived with Tracy, Ron and his cousin's family. According to a report from Northtown Social Services, who only visited once, the children were being very well looked after and both thriving. Tracy was not happy in Northtown for long, however, and had begun to spend longer and more frequent periods at her mother's house in Southtown.

In October 92 the family moved back to Southtown, this time to New Estate on the far side of town to Old Estate and Tracy's mother. Ron had reluctantly agreed, although he kept his job in Northtown. A social worker visited and was more than satisfied with the welfare of the children but did note the tension in Tracy and Ron's relationship. As no help was requested in this regard the case was closed.

The file has a note attached of a conversation with a Probation Officer, dated June 96, indicating that a welfare report had been written for the divorce court but that no further involvement was envisaged.

A further note from a Health Visitor announces the arrival of John but does not express any concern. No referral is made and so the file is not re-opened.

CURRENT SITUATION

Tracy came into the neighbourhood office on New Estate during the week saying that she was at the end of her tether and very anxious about the safety of her children.

It would seem that Alison and Michael have been spending occasional weekends and most holidays with Ron since the divorce. All has not been going well recently, however, and Alison, in particular, has been complaining to her mother that she doesn't enjoy going. She particularly dislikes the way her brother Michael is treated so differently. According to Tracy, this is becoming increasingly obvious as they are growing up. Last time the children went to stay, Michael spent most of his time with his father whereas Alison was expected to spend all her time with Ron's wife and Wayne. She found it hard, particularly as Ron's wife seemed to dote on the new baby and ignore her. Michael, on the other hand, says that he enjoys being with his father, uncles and 'new brother'.

The situation has caused a lot of arguments between Alison and Michael, which has spilled over into arguments between Tracy and Ron. Ron has said that he is unhappy with the way that the children were being brought up and that they would have a better upbringing with him and his new wife and family. He is talking about going to court to have the children live with him.

The situation at home is becoming unbearable and Tracy says that she doesn't know if she can keep going. She says it is affecting her relationship with Alun and she feels that John is getting a raw deal. Alun is not, apparently, very supportive and she feels he would probably want to see 'the back of' the two eldest. He has never liked Ron, according to Tracy, and is beginning to take it out on all of the children and on her. Tracy does not want to 'lose the children again'. She wants a social worker to come and help. Mrs. Taylor (senior) is aggravating the situation as she doesn't get on with Alun. The tension at home is rising and Tracy hinted to the duty social worker that 'something will break' if she doesn't get help.

Exercise 7.1: Getting to Know You

Note: for the purposes of this exercise, and for all of those exercises that use this case material, the sequence of events is important. In order to ensure that this book has a 'shelf-life' we have adopted a particular convention regarding dates. Days and months are given in the usual way. The current year, however, is always 100. For example, in this exercise you are asked to assume that you are reading the file in early January 100. Michael, one of the characters in the case material, is reported to have been born in June 90. This makes him $9\frac{1}{2}$ years old for the purposes of this exercise, that is it is $9\frac{1}{2}$ years from 6/90 to 1/100, from the year he was born to 'now'.

Assume that you are reading this file in January 100.

TASKS:

1. Establish the basis of this family's history in chronological order using the card index method described above.

2. Draw a flowchart for Tracy Taylor.

3. Prepare an ecomap for Alison. Include all the members of her family referred to in the case file.

4. Draw a genogram for the whole family.

QUESTIONS:

1. How old was Alison when her parents divorced?

2. How old was Ron when Alison was born?

3. How old was Alison when she was first fostered?

4. How long did John live in Northtown?

5. How old was Alison when Michael was born?

6. How old was Michael when John was born?

7. How old was Tracy when her father died?

8. How long after the birth of Michael did Tracy's father die and how long before she moved to Northtown?

9. How old was Tracy at the birth of each of her children?

10. How old is Tracy now?

11. How long was she married?

12. How old was Tracy when her parents divorced?

13. How old was she when she became pregnant?

14. How old are each of the children now?

15. What relation is Wayne to Alison?

16. Who are John's grandparents?

17. Who are Alison's grandparents?

18. How many maternal aunts/uncles does John have?

19. What relation is Alun to Wayne?

20. What relation is Alun to Alison?

Points to Consider

1. What are the key pieces of information in the file that you might want to confirm with family members?

2. Have you begun to form an idea of what gaps exist in your knowledge of this family? If so, list them.

3. From the information that you have, write down what impression you have begun to form of Alun and Ron?

4. Can you identify just how much of that impression is based on what you found in the 'file' and how much of it comes from preconceptions of your own?

5. Describe Tracy's history of involvement with your department. What might her expectations be of you and what you might do?

6. Write down what expectations you have of Tracy. Do your expectations focus on Tracy's potential weaknesses or on her strengths?

 **BOUNDARIES**

You may wish to continue to interpret the 'facts' of this case, which you should now have firmly fixed in your mind. We would suggest that there are some obvious associations between past events and the current situation that may have relevance to future work with the family. You may, of course, choose to leave any further speculation until you 'meet' the family and negotiate the nature of your involvement.

As yet, however, we have not provided you with any context in which to place this information or any other information that you may seek to collect. How do you know which pieces of information are relevant? You may have identified what you don't know, but how much more do you really need to find out? Determining which information is to be included in the assessment and which is not self-evidently defines the assessment itself and decisions made at this point will need to be justifiable and justified to all parties. Having made it clear at the outset of this Unit how difficult it is to find the beginning of an assessment, knowing where to set the boundaries looks like it might prove just as interesting a challenge.

Assessments in social work are usually intended to be functional and often derive from a specific concern – that is to say that they are usually begun because a particular decision has to be made and that decision carried into effect. This makes the boundaries on the assessment process a little easier to identify in practice than we have suggested above. Should this child be returned to the care of its parents? Should this child be removed from home? What services does this family need to ensure that the children achieve an appropriate standard of health and development? Most often, it is in response to questions such as these that assessments are undertaken.

Assessments, as well as being situational, are also theoretically informed. The thread that weaves together the 'facts' observed, their interpretation and any subsequent action may be informed by theories about how individuals think or behave in society and/or by theories about the nature and role of social work. We have suggested already that assessments are also necessarily subjective, partial and dynamic (go back to Exercise 7.1 and write down exactly on what basis you have identified certain information as 'key' in your answer to the follow up questions we asked). We will suggest in the next Unit that assessments and planning also bear the imprint of the agency and the practical context in which they are rooted. Given the number of variables that will influence the process and the immediate outcome of any assessment, we feel that it is important that you adopt a critical view of any assessment that you are likely to carry out – this includes being critical of your own role in the process, especially in so far as you determine what it is that is to be assessed.

In order to illustrate what is meant, and to introduce you to some key texts in this area, there follow three highly condensed accounts of important, contemporary frameworks for assessment. The first is a more traditional 'all-purpose' model of assessment, the second is highly specific and the third has a general application but starts with a particular focus on children looked after by the local authority. You must not rely on these accounts as sufficient to enable you to apply them directly in practice. It is strongly suggested that you read all three of them in the original. You should compare them and think about their strengths and weaknesses, how and why they might appeal to you and in what circumstances you might use them. The exercise that follows requires you to apply your conclusions to the Taylor case.

Study Text 7.2:
Three Frameworks for Assessment

'GOOD-ENOUGH PARENTING'

In 1985 the British Agencies for Adoption and Fostering (BAAF) published a modest book bearing this title (Adcock and White 1985). Proceeding
on the basis that a great many of the decisions that child and family social
workers have to make are based on judgements of parenting skills and
capacities, the book questions whether there is any kind of professional
consensus around what constitutes 'good-enough' (as opposed to both
ideal and not good-enough) parenting. The book consists of a series of
papers 'identifying the questions [that] each profession should ask and
providing aids for observation and information gathering' (p.6).

The book could be cast in the tradition of the human socialisation
theories of much child welfare thinking in the UK since the 1940s. For
example, the book's authors agreed easily that 'measurement of physical
development in young children was a good indication of satisfactory or
unsatisfactory progress' (p.6) and the checklists promised by the introduction include Sheridan's developmental progress charts and Fahlberg's
checklists on attachment behaviour in young children. There was a
disproportionate number of participants drawn from the medical (particularly the psychiatric) world at the seminar in which the book originated
and the key theoretical chapters in the final text are all authored by
eminent psychiatrists or paediatricians. The book does not adopt an
entirely 'medicalised' view of social problems, however, and does represent a serious attempt to make the theoretical assumptions and the process
of assessment as explicit as possible, particularly to the parents of the
families concerned.

In summary, the various dimensions of assessment included in this
particular model are as follows:

- the problem areas for the child or his (*sic*) upbringing which
  cause the worker and the family concern
- the environmental factors which contribute to the problem
- the level of parental and family functioning

- aspects of the family history that may be relevant to the situation
- the potential for change
- the changes that are necessary to resolve the problem.

The situational nature of this model of assessment is immediately clear. It begins with an exploration of what the current problem is and for whom. This may involve an analysis of the risks involved in a given situation or of the potential consequences of matters being allowed to take their own course. Structural poverty, physical insecurity and poor housing conditions are part of many personal problems and a consideration of the social circumstances in which the problem has arisen will also provide useful insight into the situation the family now faces. The psychological, physical and emotional development of the key actors is also a focus of interest, both in terms of understanding the current situation and in terms of planning the next step. The adults' knowledge and parenting skills might be explored through direct observation of how the family actually functions as a family. This could be expanded by a detailed consideration of the family's own history and the familial histories of the parents. If their experience of being parented is in some way impoverished or inadequate then work may be needed in this area. Finally, it will be obvious that the process of assessment in this model is seen to flow inevitably into the processes of planning and on into direct work.

Despite the age of this source, general assessments based on this or similar assumptions and theories of human behaviour, either directly or loosely, are still commonly found in social work practice.

THE 'ORANGE BOOK'

The 'Orange Book', or *Protecting Children – A Guide for Social Workers undertaking a Comprehensive Assessment* to give it its full title, was first published by the Department of Health in 1988. It can be seen to be part of a particularly strong tradition of central government guidance to local authority social services departments in the management of child protection cases. Such concern can be seen as part of a developing role for the state in 'governing the family' (Parton 1991) or as evidence of a clear commitment to the dissemination of best practice in the light of much publicised 'failures' in the systems designed to protect vulnerable children. The purpose of the Guide, which is arranged in the form of a manual, is to describe the essentials of a 'comprehensive assessment for long term planning in child protection cases' (DOH 1988, p. iii). The Guide also acknowledges that 'children and young persons are now often seen as having rights of their own, independent of their parents... Where there is a conflict of interests between the parents and the child, the child's interests must be given first consideration' (p.9). The Guide acknowledges the responsibility professionals carry to ensure open and honest communication with families and recognises the potential for harm to the child of 'dangerous professionals'. That is to say, for example, social workers and others who 'operate alone and unsupported...who act without a theoretical base and [a] systematic, structured approach to intervention' (DOH 1988, p.12).

The various components of a comprehensive assessment are as follows:

- The Causes for Concern: this includes a consideration, for example, of:
    - the type of abuse
    - direct examples of the problem
    - history of the problem
- The Child: this includes a consideration, for example, of:
    - parental perceptions of their parenting and of the child
    - the routine care of the child
    - the child's early and subsequent history
    - the child's emotional development
    - the child's growth and development
    - the child's perceptions of his/her situation, family and problems
- Family Composition
- Individual Profile of Parents/Carers: this includes a consideration, for example, of:
    - the parents' own childhood
    - reactions to stress
    - dependency
    - criminal record

112	a	How would you describe your sex life?
	b	Do you use any contraception?
	c	Do you plan to have any more children?

113	What do you like
	i	most
	ii	least about your partner?

116	Is race/culture/religion important to you in deciding the role of father, mother and other family members?
	If yes, ask the following:
	In your race/culture and/or religion what role is the father/mother expected to play in relation to:
	a	money
	b	the children
	c	work
	d	other matters
	Then ask the same questions in relation to other family members (e.g. maternal grandmother/grandfather paternal grandmother/grandfather, older and younger brothers, etc).
	Also ask whether any of the above do not fulfil their role? What do they do differently?

118	a	What are the rules – spoken or unspoken – in your family?
	b	Who makes the rules?
	c	Does anyone break them?

Figure 7.4 The 'Orange Book'

- The Couple Relationship and Family Interactions
- Social Networks
- Finance
- Physical Conditions.

The social worker using the Guide is provided with a series of questions under each heading. There are 167 questions in all, many with several sub-sections. For example, in relation to the Couple Relationship and Family Interactions section (questions 99–122), the questions in Figure 7.4 are included.

The Guide makes it clear that it was never the intention to ask parents and others exactly these questions in exactly this order. It was for the social worker to devise an appropriate form of wording. The Guide ends with advice on how to use the assessment as the basis for action planning.

ASSESSING OUTCOMES IN CHILD CARE

Professor Roy Parker and his colleagues, working around the time of the passing and implementation of the Children Act 1989, produced a suite of materials designed to systematically structure and integrate the assessment process with action planning on behalf of children. The materials include a series of age-related Assessment and Action Records that have become widely accepted as the basis of assessment and planning in key areas of childcare throughout England and Wales. Although presented with children looked after by the local authority specifically in mind, the authors envisaged the extension of their approach to include children 'in need' too.

Essentially, the process involves the systematic review of key areas of a child's life and a critical evaluation of progress made, not just by the child but also by those involved professionally in delivering services to the child/family. In this way one is able to assess 'how a local authority fulfils *all* rather than *some* of its parental responsibilities' (Parker 1991, p.35) whilst still being able to concentrate on outcomes for children. The authors examine many of the conceptual and theoretical issues that are associated with outcome measures before outlining the key 'dimensions for assessment' (p.77) that the framework includes. These are:

- Health: a parent is usually very sensitive to even small changes in a child's health, the physical nurture of a child being the 'basic parental task' (Parker 1991, p.84). For children looked after by the local authority, both this kind of intuitive knowledge as well as the more straightforward factual knowledge of the child's health record can easily be lost.

- Education/skills training: parents will sacrifice much for the sake of a child's education and its general importance to most families is evidenced by how estate agents regard proximity to good schools as a major selling point. Children in the public care will often already have come with a disrupted educational background and there is evidence, according to Parker, to suggest that the education of 'looked after' children does not receive adequate attention.

- Emotional development and behaviour: it is often emotional and behavioural problems that go beyond parents' or carers' capacity to cope that will precipitate a young person coming to be looked after by the local authority. Instability and discontinuity in care can themselves produce emotional and behavioural disturbance and so, while rarely straightforward, the persistence or reduction of such problems is a key indicator of a successful outcome for a child.

- Social, family and peer relationships: in Unit 5 we explored some of the difficulties of maintaining links for 'looked after' children and we would agree that the creation or maintenance of a 'supportive, affectionate and reliable network of relationships' (Parker 1991, p.95) with brothers and sisters, the extended family, friends and neighbours is an enormously important outcome in childcare.

- Self-care and competence: children do need to look after themselves, in every sense. They need to acquire the basic life skills of decision making, handling money, making and sustaining relationships, for example, and this is not something that can be crammed into a 12-week preparation for leaving care 'package'. It is a lifelong process that begins at birth.

- Identity: a knowledge of yourself, your history and your potential is vital to your sense of well-being. Often, 'looked after' children will have learned to take a very negative view of all three.

S1. Which of the following can the child do?	Fully mastered	Learning	Not learning	Don't know
(a)　Clean teeth without being told	☐	☐	☐	☐
(b)　Bath self	☐	☐	☐	☐
(c)　Make bed	☐	☐	☐	☐
(d)　Get a drink or snack for him/herself	☐	☐	☐	☐
(e)　Wash up	☐	☐	☐	☐
(f)　Be aware of common hazards such as poisons, tools, electricity, fires	☐	☐	☐	☐
(g)　Answer the telephone	☐	☐	☐	☐
(h)　Make an emergency telephone call	☐	☐	☐	☐
(i)　Handle small amounts of money	☐	☐	☐	☐
(j)　Cross quiet roads safely	☐	☐	☐	☐

In the case of skills not being taught or lack of information

Who will take further action?

☐ Parent　　　　☐ Social Worker　　☐ Foster Carer
☐ Residential Worker　☐ Other　　　☐ No action needed

Explanation for lack of information or no action

Figure 7.5 Assessment action record

- Social presentation: social attractiveness does matter. Children are likely to be shunned on account of their 'unattractive appearance, unlikeable personal habits and inappropriate social behaviour' (Parker 1991, p.100), particularly by other children.

Parker and his team are at pains to point out how the several components within the framework interact and reinforce each other. Poor social presentation is likely to reinforce social isolation, which may lower self-esteem, which will, in turn, affect school performance, which may produce behavioural difficulties, and so on. The standards against which the assessment is made, in the case of the local authority's responsibilities, is that of the 'reasonable parent' and, in the case of the child, the 'norms that are prevalent in the general population' (Parker 1991, p.36). This is, perhaps, best illustrated by reference to an early version of the Assessment Action Record for 5–9-year-olds (Figure 7.5). The extract is taken from the section dealing with Self-Care Skills.

Whilst each of the models of assessment described above was designed with a particular purpose in mind and each is located in a different practice context and was developed at a different time, there are some clear correspondences. There are differences too. In the following exercise we want you to compare and contrast these and any other models of assessment that you know of and answer some key questions.

Exercise 7.2: Contrasts

Comparing each of the thumbnail accounts of particular models of assessment presented in Study Text 7.2, and any other models of assessment that you have read about or seen in practice, make a list of similarities and differences using the following headings as a starting point:

1. Implied theory(ies) of human behaviour.

2. Implied theory(ies) of social work.

3. Required knowledge base.

4. Implied mode of information gathering.

5. Type of information sought.

6. Range of information sought.

7. Volume of information sought.

8. Implied role of social worker.

9. Implied role of child.

10. Implied role of parent/carer.

Points to Consider

1. How important is it in any assessment to identify and differentiate the interests of all the parties to the process?

2. How far can assessment frameworks accommodate race and class differences as well as variations in family form and household structures?

3. How easy might it be to maintain the mutuality of the assessment process with participants who are under investigation in some way or who are party to the process against their will?

4. What might be the consequences of adopting an inquisitorial style in any assessment?

5. What are the advantages and disadvantages of 'checklists' in the assessment process?

6. What might be the consequences of collecting too much information?

STANDARDS

Perhaps the most important stage of all in the assessment process is the evaluation of the information gathered. Against what standards are you to judge what you find? Each of the models described in Study Text 7.2 seem to imply a consensus articulated by Parker as the 'norms that are prevalent in the general population' (Parker 1991, p. 36) but, as we have suggested throughout this book, few 'norms' can be taken for granted. To take a trivial example: on what class/cultural/gender basis ought we to judge the appropriateness of doing the washing-up as a suitable measure of 'self care and competence' amongst 5–9 year olds? (See the extract from Parker's Assessment Action Record in Figure 7.5). On a more serious level, what is the 'right answer' to questions about one's sex life or one's choice of contraception? (See Question 112 in extract from 'Orange Book' in Figure 7.4).

It is not our intention to provide you with answers to questions of this sort but we do believe that it is vital for you to be able to provide answers for yourselves. The next exercise is designed to encourage you to demonstrate that you can do so in practice.

Exercise 7.3: Beginning the Assessment

Due to pressure of work, you have not been able to go out and see the Taylor Family yet but the family did come back into the office during the week. You were not available and Tracy was seen by a senior colleague of yours. Mrs Taylor was threatening to have all of the children placed in care. Your colleague managed to diffuse the situation but his/her report adds nothing to your knowledge of the family. However, the report concludes that, as the situation is so messy and complicated and so obviously highly charged, a full assessment of the family should be made. Your Team Leader thinks that this would be a good idea too.

TASKS:

1. Devise a framework for the assessment of this family.

2. Your framework must include a full account of the headings (dimensions of assessment) under which you will gather information and include a detailed list of the kind (but not necessarily the form) of questions to which you will be seeking answers.

3. For at least *two* of the broad headings under which you will be gathering information, set out your reasons for asking the kind of questions that you intend. Your reasons must include a reference to the theoretical perspective that you are adopting.

4. For at least *one* of the headings under which you will be gathering information, give examples of the responses that might cause you concern.

Points to Consider

1. Is there information that you consider essential to all assessments?

2. Are you able to justify asking for all of the information that you intend to gather?

3. How would you explain to Tracy why you were asking for the information that you are seeking?

4. How might you interpret a refusal to provide information?

5. Other than direct questioning, what other information gathering skills or techniques might you use?

6. How well able are you to articulate the standards against which you will be judging the information you gather?

CONCLUSION

We have only hinted at the practicalities of undertaking an assessment of any sort and said even less of the agency context in which it will take place. Our intention has been to encourage and enable you to reflect upon the *process* of assessment and to recognise that it is a negotiated one. There are many different routes to 'make sense of what has happened and of what is happening now'. Assessment is the foundation for planning and so for direct work but it is an interpretative process throughout. What areas are selected for assessment, what information is gathered and the criteria against which information is evaluated remain open questions. We have not argued for a particular form or model of assessment but we do believe that you must be in a position to articulate and defend any one that you might use.

NOTES AND SELF-ASSESSMENT

1. How would you explain to a ten-year-old what you mean by 'assessment'?

2. How comfortable are you articulating the theories that inform your work?

3. Who should 'own' the assessment?

4. How easy to assess are you?

5. How would you feel about being assessed by a social worker? Write down why you feel as you do.

6. What aspects of your own life or personal history would you find most difficult to introduce into an assessment being made of you?

RECOMMENDED READING

Adcock, M. and White, R. (eds) (1985) *Good-enough Parenting – a Framework for Assessment.* London: BAAF.

Parker, R., Ward, H., Jackson, S., Aldgate, J. and Wedge, P. (1991) *Assessing Outcomes in Child Care.* London: HMSO.

DOH (1988) *Protecting Children – A Guide for Social Workers Undertaking a Comprehensive Assessment.* London: HMSO.

TRAINER'S NOTES

Exercise 7.1: Getting To Know You

Task 1 is best done individually as each member of the group will need a thorough knowledge of the 'file' for subsequent work. Tasks 2, 3 and 4 are best distributed amongst the group – the resulting material can then be shared with other group members and retained for use in later sessions. This works well if the material is prepared using flipchart paper. The 'twenty questions' can be used to test the group's knowledge of the case after a simple reading of the file (i.e. before attempting any of the tasks) and then again after the tasks have been completed. This is usually a powerful demonstration of how much information can be gleaned from only a few pages after a little less than an hour's work. We have deliberately not supplied any answers to the questions as we do not want anyone (including the trainer) to take a short cut to a working knowledge of the case.

Ignoring information gaps, forming impressions based on personal prejudices or over-emphasis on weaknesses and the priorities of the worker are common faults amongst newly qualified workers and group members should be encouraged to illustrate the discussion with material drawn from their own experience.

Exercise 7.2: Contrasts

Ideally, group members will have read, at least between them, all three models of assessment described in Study Text 7.2 before attempting this exercise. One very useful way into the exercise is to present Howe's well-known taxonomy of social work (1987). This gives group members a very helpful vocabulary with which to discuss the issues that arise. In practice, headings 1 and 2 can be taken together, 4–7 and 8–10 similarly, and discussed in sub-groups before presentation to the whole group.

Exercise 7.3: Beginning the Assessment

This exercise is intended as a summarising or re-enforcing exercise. It can be used most effectively to integrate practice and classroom study if, instead of preparing an assessment schedule using the Taylor case, a real case from group members' own experience or current practice is used. This can be combined with a skills rehearsal exercise around the presentation of formal assessments. Instructions can be given as follows:

> This exercise is intended to provide opportunities for you to share your practice experience with your colleagues and to benefit from the practice experience of others; to encourage you to reflect on the relevant skills that you possess or need to develop; to provide you with an opportunity to rehearse your skills in communicating your assessments to others.
>
> For the (next) session prepare a five minute presentation (*no more and no less*) of a case or incident of which you have direct knowledge that has involved you in the process of assessment of a particular child or family situation.
>
> Structure your presentation as follows:
>
> 1. Describe the particular situation and circumstances that gave rise to the assessment that you made and some indication of what conclusions you have or are beginning to form about the child/situation.
>
> 2. *Either* identify the skills that you used in making the assessment *or* describe any particular technique(s) that you used that might be of interest to your colleagues.
>
> 3. Identify what this piece of work has taught you about assessment that you would want to pass on to others.

UNIT 8
Planning

OBJECTIVES

In this unit you will:

- Consider the relationship between assessment and planning.
- Learn about the process of goal setting.
- Learn about the statutory basis for planning in childcare.
- Explore the use of written agreements in childcare.

 **WONDERLAND**

Even if you don't know the story of Alice in Wonderland, you may have heard of the Cheshire Cat. Alice is lost in the wood and is anxious to find her way out. She sees the Cheshire Cat sitting in a tree and decides to ask his advice. She asks him which way she ought to go. He replies that it rather depends on where exactly she wants to get to. Alice says that she doesn't much mind where that is, at which point the Cat interrupts and tells her that it doesn't matter which path she takes then. Alice completes her question '...so long as I get somewhere.' 'Oh you are sure to do that', replies the Cheshire Cat, 'if you only walk long enough'.

Alice's uncertainty about where she is now, her sense of urgency to get 'somewhere' and her apparent unconcern for just where that 'somewhere' turns out to be are familiar feelings for many social work practitioners. What Alice needs is a plan! Not just a two-dimensional map of Wonderland, although with that she could at least work out which paths lead where, she would know a little better where she had been and what might be waiting around the next corner. Her progress through Wonderland would, at least from that point on, be a more rational and predictable one.

A simple map wouldn't help her decide her destination, however, and it wouldn't necessarily tell her who she would meet on the way or of any new short-cuts or hold-ups; for that she would need to use knowledge drawn from her experience in the wood, and elsewhere, and be certain of her purpose. She would need to make a series of decisions that would take her further towards where she wanted to be – she would have to engage in a *process* of rational and purposive decision making to really make progress through the wood. It is this process of rational, purposive decision making, or planning, that is the subject of this Unit.

To give a more practical illustration, consider the point at which the previous Unit on assessment ended. Once the framework for your assessment has been decided and you have begun to flesh out the substantive areas that you want the assessment to cover (see Exercise 7.3), you then have to think about the actual process of carrying it out. There are a number of questions you will need to consider at this point: who are you going to consult? Who will you want to speak to in person? In what order will you see people? Where will you meet them? Who will you see together and who separately? What would be a good time to see the children? After school? What if that conflicts with meal times for the children? And so on.

You could simply answer each question as it arose and proceed on that basis. You may even be able to complete an assessment in this way. People do. There is considerable evidence (DHSS 1985; DOH 1991c) to suggest that a great deal of childcare social work proceeds in a planning vacuum. Alternatively, you could organise, prioritise and take positive decisions about what you will do and *plan* the assessment. If assessment is about 'making sense of what has happened and what is happening now', planning is about making sense of what will happen next.

Assessments need to be planned, but the relationship between assessment and planning is not an easy one to define. The boundary between planning more generally and direct work is frequently indistinct. Indeed, planning is described as occurring at subtly different stages depending on which particular model of social work practice you choose.

Siporin (1975) has it rather neatly following assessment and before intervention. Compton and Galaway (1984), in their problem solving model, locate planning as occurring in the phase they describe as 'from initial contact through assessment'. Hepworth and Larsen (1982) locate planning within the assessment phase which precedes the 'change orientated phase.' Volume 4 of the Guidance and Regulations that accompany the Children Act 1989 notes that: 'Chronologically, the planning process should comprise the following typical stages: inquiry, consultation, assessment and decision making' (DOH 1991d, para.2.43).

Clearly, we need to retain a degree of flexibility around those activities that we associate particularly, if not exclusively, with planning. In fact, much like assessment, planning is a continuous process in need of constant review and up-dating and one which overlaps with other phases in the social work process. But, accepting that planning can not be easily divorced from other elements in the social work process, what can we say about beginning to plan and how that relates to assessment?

Planning begins with the identification of the planning required, with the question 'planning for what?' – the answer to which can only derive from the nature of the assessment that is underway. Usually, during the assessment stage, some preliminary decisions must be taken about the immediate future and about the expected direction of events later on. Indeed, in an emergency, decisions often have to be made and action taken before the situation can be even partially assessed. But, these kind of situational responses are not plans in the sense in which we intend; this would imply that planning is far too reactive a process. Planning is itself a form of causality, it is about *making* things happen rather than simply responding to events as they occur. So, while planning is inextricably bound up with the assessment phase (assessments need to planned too), it is not coterminous with it. While the assessment phase may well be on-going and may well be revisited and revised during the course of the social work involvement, there is a very general sense in which it is concerned with what has happened or is happening now. Planning is about what happens next – understood in the instrumental sense of what is intended *should* happen next. Understood in this way, planning rests upon decision making directed towards a desired end or goal.

Volume 4 of the Guidance and Regulations that accompany the Children Act 1989 develops this point and has described planning as involving (DOH 1991d, para. 2.60):

- translating the assessed needs into goals and objectives

- listing and appraising the specific options available (or which may need to be created) for achieving these objectives

- deciding on the preferred option, setting out the reasons for the decision.

The core social work process of goal setting is the subject of Study Text 8.1.

Study Text 8.1: Goal Setting

What do we mean when we use the term 'goal'? Amongst the definitions offered by the Shorter Oxford Dictionary, two seem particularly apt for our purposes: 'Goal: the object of effort or ambition, or the destination of a (difficult) journey'.

In a social work context, Hepworth and Larsen (1982) note that goals serve the following valuable functions in the helping process:

- goals provide direction and continuity to the helping process and prevent needless wandering

- goals facilitate the development and selection of appropriate strategies and interventions

- goals assist practitioners and clients to monitor their progress

- goals serve as outcome criteria in evaluating the effectiveness of specific interventions and the helping process.

Moreover, it is suggested that the process of goal setting with service users contributes substantially to the effectiveness of the helping process itself. Goal setting is motivational. Knowing that there is at least the possibility of arriving somewhere beyond the circumstances that prompted the initial contact can often bring a renewed sense of optimism and confidence for both service user and worker.

What kind of appropriate 'destinations' might be defined as goals? Goals are not to be expressed in global terms. They cannot be generalised to the level of life, the universe and everything. To be useful, goals must remain specific to the current person/situational circumstances. Hence statements like 'to make X better', 'happier' or 'better able to cope' are not goals so much as pious intentions. Goals must reflect the nature of the issues that originated the helping process in the first place, for example 'to improve the quality of parenting', 'to increase participation in social groups', 'to improve verbal communication' or 'to relate more comfortably with the opposite sex'. In this way, goal statements, although somewhat abstract, are still rooted in the circumstances (person/situation dynamic) that brings the social worker and the service user together. Goals expressed at this level of generality should be distinguished from objectives or aims which Anderson (1984) describes as 'statements of intended accomplishments that are specific, attainable, appropriate and measurable' (p.488). In other words, objectives are the steps we take along the path to reaching our goals.

A well constructed objective statement will answer the five key questions of who, what, to what extent, when and where:

1. WHO? The objective statement is often made with reference to the service user. This does not necessarily imply that the identified service user is the only object of any objective statement. For example, if the social worker is engaged with a family it is important to specify whether the objective is to be attained by all family members, specific family members or by others altogether, including representatives of outside agencies.

2. WHAT? The task here is to formulate statements that are specific to the desired outcome. For example, such a statement as 'To get Chris to attend school' is inadequate. Does that mean just once more or every day for the next two terms? Without this degree of specificity, how can one begin to evaluate progress? To blur this distinction between specific outcomes and more generalised statements of intent can be very tempting. To promise a court 'To get Chris to attend school' leaves plenty of room for negotiation if at any point you have to report back. It also lets you off the hook in other ways in that lack of specificity allows you to set, in effect, very low-level objectives. Getting Chris to attend school once in the next two years may satisfy your objective statement but it does little for Chris's educational development.

3. TO WHAT EXTENT? Answers to this question do not have to be set only in positivistic, numerical terms. Other formulations are possible: for example, 'to stop sniffing solvents on my own' describes a specific context rather than any quantitative element. But, whether expressed in qualitative or quantitative terms or any combination of them, the message is one of specificity.

4. WHEN? This question addresses when the expected outcome is going to occur. The time frame will need to be realistic in order to achieve a balance between motivation and setting a course for inevitable and avoidable 'failure' judged by not meeting arbitrary deadlines.

5. WHERE? Often, problematic behaviours occur in specific settings or at specified times during the day. Answering this question of the objective statement tells everyone where to look for the expected outcome.

It should be noted that despite the apparent deterministic approach reflected in the above, the goal setting process is a mutual one. Just as with assessment, goal setting is not something done to clients by social workers (a particular way of ensuring the mutuality of the goal setting process is the subject of Study Text 8.3). However, in order for you to practice what is involved in the goal setting phase of the planning process, we want to return to the Taylor Family, to catch up on events and to begin the process of planning with them.

Taylor Family Case File

It is now towards the end of January. You have been able to make just a brief introductory visit to the family since receiving the referral. This means that, unfortunately, you have not been able to really get going on any kind of comprehensive assessment. Indeed, you have been overtaken by events once more, as the following case notes reveal:

The weekend following your last visit, Ron came down to collect Alison and Michael. Alison refused to go. There was a very heated discussion on the doorstep, which ended in a fight between Alun and Ron. Ron eventually left without the children, who had witnessed the fight and who were very distressed. On the Sunday, Alun and Tracy also came to blows over the situation and Tracy left with the three children and has gone to stay with her mother. You have visited Mrs Taylor's (senior) house and spoken to Tracy and the children.

She is adamant that she will not go home to Alun and does not want to try and remove him from the family home at this point. The tenancy is in his name. Unfortunately, she is aware also that she cannot stay where she is indefinitely as the children are already getting on their grand-mother's nerves and the tension is beginning to mount. Tracy feels that she could manage John but cannot cope with Alison and Michael, who have not stopped quarrelling since they arrived at Tracy's mother's house. Michael blames Alison for what has happened and is being very loud and aggressive. Alison is being very sullen and keeps bursting into tears.

You have already phoned Ron but he has made it clear that he cannot have Alison and Michael stay with him, except at weekends. Wayne has been poorly over recent weeks and his wife has been very upset at what happened over the weekend. His family have advised him to consult a solicitor to resume the formal care of the children but he is clearly reluctant to do so. He is prepared to talk about the children and does want to see that they are well looked after. At the moment, he cannot offer accommo-dation.

Tracy is asking that the older children 'get looked after by a foster family' for a while until things settle down. You have contacted the placement unit and they have told you that they do have two 'short-term beds' with the Williams family. The Williams', who run a small-holding, live about six miles out of Southtown. The only other option is to place the children in a residential unit, Brummell Drive. This is a small unit, due for closure shortly, that is more used to dealing with older children.

You have not had very much time to get to know the children, as yet. Michael does appear to be very fond of his father and protective of both Alison and John. His relationship with his mother is being tested but you feel that there is a strong bond. He is probably appearing braver than he feels at the moment. You know that he is doing very well at school and is very keen on football and his computer games.

Alison, although older than Michael, seems emotionally much less mature. She is very 'clingy' with mother and seems to think that dad is trying to break them up. She seems resentful of John. Both children speak very harshly of Alun, who they are clearly in no hurry to see again.

John is very quiet for his age and seems to you to be developmentally delayed. He has very little language and is still in nappies. You have been meaning to have a word with the health visitor but have not been able to yet. You were beginning to be worried about him before this last episode occurred and recent events have not lessened your concern.

Mrs Taylor (senior) is blaming the whole world for what is happening and switches from being very aggressive towards you, Tracy and the children to utterly indifferent. She leaves you in no doubt whatsoever that the children cannot stay with her. Tracy and her mother insist on foster care for the children. She will not allow them to go to any of her brothers and sisters as 'most of them have got social workers already'. Mrs Taylor (senior) tells you bluntly 'I know what is right for my grandchildren and I know that you have to listen to what I say. I want them fostered for a week or two till we can get things sorted out'. In the circumstances, you are inclined to agree.

Exercise 8.1: Goal Setting

Using the framework for assessment developed as part of Exercise 7.3, but adding relevant information contained in these case notes, begin to plan for the immediate future of these children. You should assume that the children will need to be looked after by the local authority for a period. In particular:

1. Identify clearly what it is you are planning for and prepare statements of the goals you intend your plans to achieve.

2. Identify the specific objectives that you intend to achieve on the way to the overall goals that you have determined.

Points to Consider

1. Have you included goal statements in respect of where the children will live and who will parent them?

2. How well do you think your goals will meet the needs of the children?

3. How well do you think your goals will meet the wishes and feelings of the children?

4. How well have you reflected the needs, wishes and feelings of all the adults involved in the goals you have chosen?

5. Are you able to answer the five basic questions in relation to each objective (Who, What, To What Extent, When and Where)?

6. Are your statements of objectives 'specific, attainable, appropriate and measurable'?

THE CONTEXT OF PLANNING

Unlike the fictional world in which Alice had to make her way, planning in social work takes place in an immensely complex and variable context in which a number of elements may have a bearing on both the planning process and its outcomes. For example, the 'culture' and structure of the agency in which you are working can have a direct bearing on how you approach planning generally. It can be very easy, as Menzies (1970) pointed out in relation to child protection, for example, for any group of professionals to develop relationships, systems of belief (or, more properly, 'systems of disbelief') or particular 'practice cultures' to serve as defences against the anxieties and stresses of the work. These systems of belief can include very firm ideas of 'how we do things here', which may be entirely unproductive as far as service users are concerned. The volume of work you are expected to deal with and the degree of professional support and supervision that you routinely receive are other examples of how agency context can determine your capacity to plan adequately.

Your capacity to plan is also clearly influenced by your own professional skill and knowledge. You cannot plan for what you do not know or, more positively, the more extensive your repertoire of interventive techniques, the more alternatives you might be able to build into your direct work. Of course, your plans will be influenced by the resources at your disposal more generally, including those provided by agencies other than your own.

Certain planning goals can be subject to particular, or more general, disapproval, depending on the local or national political context in which you work. At times, alternatives to custody for juveniles, for example, have been broadly supported. At others, they have been reviled. The professional credibility of social work and social workers ebbs and flows and certain interventions or risk thresholds are supported at certain times, with certain user groups and in certain places, and at others they are not.

Your plans are made in the context of countless other plans made by other individuals and other organisations. But do not feel that any of the elements that we have described as forming the context of planning are immune from the planning process or that your plans are necessarily entirely determined by external considerations. Even where social workers operate in accordance with 'strict' agency policies, variations do occur. You may think of social work agencies operating as strongly hierarchical organisations with line-management structures organised as a pyramid: the Director at the top and you somewhere near the bottom. Such structures are said to have more or less strongly centralised decision and policy-making structures and procedures. However, as each agency is largely composed of professionally-trained people, or those who aspire to professional status and who rely on personal judgements, in fact, real executive power and decision making is dispersed amongst those operating at the 'front line'. Workers on the front line tend to be grouped in units, which are, in fact, dispersed more in the manner of spokes on a wheel rather than as the broad base of a pyramid.

In this way front line units have considerable scope for recreating and redefining agency policy and practice by the way in which they decide to order priorities, initiate new work and set objectives in their day-to-day work with service users. Front line units, it is argued (Smith 1965), can acquire a high degree of autonomy, both from the centre and from each other – that is to say that the agency's policy is created from the countless small decisions that are taken at the front line rather than something which is generated at the top and disseminated downwards through the agency. Differing professional thresholds of 'good enough parenting' amongst individual social workers, for example, may more strongly influence the rate at which children are looked after by the local authority than any chief officer-led strategy to reduce admissions to residential care. In such organisations the main problem of the organisational parent is one of control and it will usually seek to introduce a variety of regulatory and standardising procedures (e.g. case conferences). But their effect can be overstated. It is these variations in the context of planning that, in part, account for the enormous variety in social work practice from agency to agency and across the country.

There is one element of the context of planning, however, that has been established explicitly as a unifying set of principles and practices: namely the Children Act 1989. We have seen at several points in this book already how the Act frequently provides the immediate context for practice in this field. As well as the Act itself, the statutory Regulations and Guidance that accompany it can greatly influence the form and content of direct work. Without wishing to influence the plans you have begun to formulate for the Taylor Family, you may have recognised that you will shortly have to plan for the children being looked after by someone other than Tracy. The following Study Text is intended to locate your planning with the Taylor Family in the context of Guidance and Regulations.

Note: Before you read the following Study Text you may wish to re-read Study Text 5.3, which deals with the general duties that a local authority has in relation to a child that it is, or is proposing to, look after.

Study Text 8.2: Planning for Children Looked After by the Local Authority

THE ARRANGEMENTS FOR PLACEMENT OF CHILDREN (GENERAL) REGULATIONS 1991

These Regulations require the agency proposing to place a child (the 'responsible authority') to make 'immediate and long-term arrangements' ('plans') for the placement and for 'promoting the welfare of the child who is to be placed' (Reg.3 (1)). This should be done before the placement or as soon as practicable thereafter. The Guidance makes it clear that 'planning is required from the earliest possible time after recognition of need or referral' (DOH 1991a and d, para.2.9). Guidance further notes that planning will achieve its purpose of safeguarding and promoting the child's welfare in so far as 'the drawing up of an individual plan for each child looked after will prevent drift and help to focus work with the family and child' (DOH 1991a and d, para.2.20).

Plans are to be recorded in writing (Reg.3(5)) and notification made to those with whom the authority consulted before making the placement under s.22(4) of the Act. In addition, the district health authority, the local education authority and the child's GP (amongst others – see Reg. 5 (1)) should be notified. Schedule 1 of the Regulations lists matters to be considered by the responsible authority when drawing up its plans. These include:

- the discharge of any existing care order or other change in a child's legal status
- arrangements for contact
- the authority's longer term plans for the child, which should include a consideration of alternative courses of action and preparation for when the child will no longer be looked after by the authority and whether plans need to be made to find a permanent substitute family for the child
- whether an independent visitor should be appointed for the child.

Remember, however, that these considerations are not intended to be exclusive and do not repeat matters already covered in the Act and noted above.

The Regulations also require the authority to arrange for a medical examination for the child and to obtain a written report of the child's 'state of health...and his need for health care' (Reg.7). A child over the age of 16 must give his or her own consent to such an examination. Younger children may also be judged competent (by the doctor) to refuse consent (DOH 1991a, para.2.32). In making its arrangements, the authority must then have regard not only to the child's current state of health and health history but to their effects on his development and any remedial, preventive or protective measure that should be taken (Schedule 2). In relation to the child's education, the authority must have regard to achieving continuity and identifying and acting upon any educational need that the child may have.

Additionally, Schedule 4 of the Regulations makes specific provisions for children who are to be accommodated but who are not in care. The Schedule requires a statement of 'any services to be provided for the child' (sch.4, para.1). It also requires clarification of the respective roles of the authority, the child's parents and those with parental responsibility –

particularly in relation to any delegation of parental responsibility (sch.4, para.4), decision making (sch.4, para.5) and contact (sch.4, para.6). The Schedule also requires that the parties consider 'the expected duration of arrangements and the steps which should apply to bring the arrangements to an end, including arrangements for the rehabilitation of the child with the person with whom he was living before the voluntary arrangements were made...' (sch.4, para.9).

THE REVIEW OF CHILDREN'S CASES REGULATIONS 1991

These Regulations establish the timing, form and core content of the review of looked after children's cases.

An initial review must take place within four weeks of a child beginning to be looked after by a responsible authority (Reg. 3 (1)). The second review should then be carried out no later than three months after the first, with subsequent reviews carried out at six monthly intervals (Reg. 3 (2)). Responsible authorities are required to set out in writing how reviews are to be carried out and to inform the child, his parents and anyone else with parental responsibility or who has a relevant interest in the review of the procedures (Regs. 4 and 7). Where 'reasonably practical', the authority should consult and involve in the review those whom it has a duty to inform, including inviting the attendance of 'persons in relation to any particular matter which is to be considered in the course of the review' (Reg. 7 (2)). Guidance makes it clear that 'only in exceptional cases should a parent or child not be invited to a review meeting' (DOH 1991a, para.8.10; see also DOH 1991d, para.3.10)

In the review, the responsible authority has to consider all of those matters set out in Schedules 1 and 2 of the Arrangements for the Placement of Children's Regulations (repeated in Schedules 2 and 3 of these Regulations) concerning the child's general and health needs and consider the child's 'educational needs, progress and development' and any special educational needs (sch.1, paras. 7 and 4).

THE FOSTER PLACEMENT (CHILDREN) REGULATIONS 1991

Although largely concerned with the approval of foster carers and the supervision of placements, which are beyond our immediate concern in this Unit, there are certain elements of these Regulations that may have a bearing on planning for the Taylor children.

Regulation 5 (1) prevents the placement of a child in a foster home unless the responsible authority is satisfied that this is 'the most suitable way' of performing their duty to safeguard and promote his welfare and that 'placement with the particular foster parent is the most suitable placement having regard to all the circumstances'. In particular, the authority are to secure that 'where possible' the foster parent is of the same religion as the child or gives an undertaking that the child will be brought up according to his or her religious persuasion.

Placements cannot be made (except in an emergency) without a written agreement between the foster carers and the authority. Matters to be dealt with in such agreements cover such practical issues as the financial support of the child, matters of consent for medical or dental treatment, arrangements for contact and permission to live, even temporarily, away from the foster parent's home (sch. 3, paras. 2, 3, 4 and 6). They must also contain a 'statement containing all the information which the authority considers necessary to enable the foster parents to care for the child'. In particular, this statement must contain details of the authority's 'arrangements for the child and the objectives of the placement' (sch. 3, para.1(a)).

Exercise 8.2: Planning For Placement

In the event, the only placement available for the Taylor children is with the Williams Family.

1. Review your plans for Alison and Michael and revise as necessary. Your review should include a consideration of all of those matters required by the Children Act 1989 and associated Regulations and Guidance.

2. Set out the sequence of events that will be necessary to put your plans into effect.

3. Using the diary sheet (Figure 8.1) below, construct a timetable to operate alongside the plan that indicates the order in which tasks (including consultations and notifications) will be undertaken.

4. Prepare a statement for the foster carers, as required by Regulations.

	Week 1	Week 2	Week 3	Week 4
M				
T				
W				
Th.				
F				
Sat				
Sun				

Week 5
Week 6
Week 7
Week 8
Week 9
Week 10
Week 11
Week 12

Month 4
Month 5
Month 6
Month 7
Month 8
Month 9
Month 10
Month 11
Month 12

Figure 8.1: Diary sheets

Points to Consider

1. What are the specific goals and objectives that your plan sets out to achieve?

2. What are the main tasks that a) the foster carers, b) the parents and c) the social worker need to undertake in order to achieve these goals and objectives?

3. Is the time-scale that you have determined appropriate to those goals and objectives?

4. What contingency plans have you made and does everyone know what these are?

5. What help do a) the foster carers, b) the parents and c) the children need to prepare for the admission?

6. Who will be responsible for, and involved in, planning for these children's longer term future?

PLANNING TOGETHER

We have made several references to the mutuality of the planning (and assessment) process. One way in which a commitment to such forms of practice can be given effect is through the use of written agreements with service users. Often, such agreements are described as 'contracts', although we would suggest that such a term should be avoided as too legalistic and possibly too intimidating for all concerned – it may remind partners of experiences that they would rather forget and be suggestive of an adversarial stance. White (1983) suggests that the intentions behind such arrangements are best conveyed by the term 'agreed planning document'. Sheldon (1980, p.2) defines written agreements as: 'agreements between social workers and their clients for the purpose of giving greater definition or sense of direction to working relationships'. He goes on to say that their usefulness lies in the way that they are able to specify who is to do what and so act as a 'continual reminder of the agreed goals and purposes of the intervention.'

Written agreements clearly offer the potential for shared work, shared responsibility, common goals and clear expectations. They do not constitute a guarantee of improved practice, however. If they are no more than a set of tasks that the service user has to carry out, with no prior negotiation and no reciprocal commitment and obligations on the social worker, then they are only of negative value. We can begin to explore their potential for positive practice by reference to what it is that families say they want from a written agreement. The following Study Text begins with such an exploration.

Study Text 8.3: Written Agreements

Based on the work of Atherton and Dowling (1989), we can identify 10 preconditions for the effective use of written agreements:

1. *The social worker's/agency's motivation must be pro-service user.* Written agreements that are intended to serve other than the explicit purposes of helping the service user to overcome the present difficulties are unlikely to prove effective. For example, a written agreement that deals with the quality of parenting but which is no more than an evidence gathering device for a forthcoming court appearance is not an agreement in any meaningful sense. This sort of negative attitude simply increases suspicion and sets an unbridgeable gap between the worker and the family. Families need to feel and believe that what is being agreed is being done so in order to help them reach their goals, with your assistance, rather than introduce a series of increasingly difficult obstacles against which to measure almost inevitable failure.

2. *Agreements should be negotiated, not imposed:* Given that we usually find what we are looking for, if you are genuinely committed to negotiating agreement you will be surprised by how often agreement can be reached. If you begin with the expectation that

agreement cannot be reached, then of course it will not be. There will be occasions when agreement between the various parties cannot be reached and often it will be you who will be called upon to make a decision. But, the distinction between what is unilaterally decided and what is negotiated must be made. Any blurring of this distinction will do nothing to establish the engagement of the family in the helping process or to establish any form of trust.

3. *All parties can take advice.* In reality, of course, social workers do take advice throughout the process. We are usually less comfortable when service users do the same. This may be interpreted as a threat to the social worker's competence or authority; to the comfortable and comforting illusion that we know best. You will almost always have access to colleagues and a variety of forms of professional advice. For families, advice may come from a friend or relative or their own solicitor. It is the worker's job to encourage, rather than frustrate, the participation of such advisers in the process and to view their presence positively. The very important principle of confidentiality is often used spuriously to discourage the involvement of other family or community members in the helping process. The role of third parties is particularly important if there is a cultural or linguistic gap to bridge.

4. *The family's view is genuinely respected.* There is all the difference in the world between listening to a family's view and hearing a family's view and between hearing a family's view and respecting it. Respecting it means giving it value and allowing the possibility that you will be at least as influenced in the direction of the family's view of the problem as you are by your own views. It is at the heart of negotiation and is a process of compromise.

5. *Agency tasks must be clearly defined.* Essentially, this is a further comment on the lack of specificity in most social work interventions consequent upon the absence of planning and any sense of what the purposes of intervention are. Too many written agreements are little more than sets of tasks for the service user to perform, with the expectations of the worker and their agency left largely unarticulated.

6. *The agreement will both be followed and reviewed.* To begin the process of intervention with the written agreement and to see it rapidly

confined to the recesses of the case file is to add insult to injury. In jettisoning the agreement unilaterally, you also jettison any expectation you might have of the co-operation of the family.

7. *The agency is willing to reconsider whether both the terms and implementation of the agreement were fair.* Written agreements can never become tablets of stone – the contents of which can never be changed, even if they have demonstrably failed in some way. The agency, as much as the service user, should be prepared to look at its own role in determining the reasons for any particular outcome.

8. *The final written document is agreed by all:* This is a point about checking out that the *written* agreement is actually the agreement that has been made and that the scribe of the written contract has not subtly, or otherwise, misconstrued or mis-represented the agreement.

9. *It is written in clear unambiguous language.* There is evidence to suggest that when social workers and other professionals are themselves uncertain of what they mean, or they wish to disguise the true content of their communication, they will use professional jargon and other devices to ensure that their status remains unquestioned and, so, unthreatened.

10. *Its contents can be appealed against.* This is clearly related to point 7 and, in the case of services for children and families, has now been given some statutory force in that each local authority is required to have in place an appropriate complaints and representations procedure (CA 1989, s.26).

Taking these points together, we can see how a written agreement can provide a base for open and honest communication between families and social workers and occupy a particular role in relationship to the planning process in that it;

- promotes explicit decision making on the part of parents, social workers, children and other collaborating persons or agencies

- specifies time frames for decision making

- ensures clarity of tasks, goals and objectives for clients, workers and others

- provides the basis of periodic review.

In terms of the kinds of cases in which written agreements might be used, there is no reason why agreements should be considered in only very restricted circumstances or only at particular points in your involvement with the family. Written agreements can, for example, take the form of:

- a preliminary statement focusing on general or broad themes and formulated early in the contact with a family
- a more definitive agreement reached after adequate discussion and review with a family and others who may be involved
- a partial agreement delineating in further detail a section of a more general agreement.

Given the variety of specific and general purposes to which an agreement might be put, it is difficult to generalise about their specific form and content. Each agreement should be seen as a unique document that flows from, and is adapted to, the particular needs and circumstances of the service user. However, there are certain components of an agreement that will be required in most situations:

- participants in the agreement
- a statement of commitment to the agreement
- a time frame for the agreement
- a statement of the goals and objectives of the plan
- specification of the tasks that will need to be undertaken by the parties to the agreement
- arrangements for periodic review
- appropriate signatures.

And what happens if one party fails to keep to the agreement? This question is often put in terms of 'where are the teeth in a written agreement?' To put this question is often to miss the point altogether. If the agreement is not honoured then it needs to be re-negotiated or, if this is not possible, it may need to be withdrawn and one or other of the parties act independently. The social worker may seek recourse to the court or a family may relinquish their relationship with the agency (if they have a choice), for example.

In so far as written agreements reflect the worker's ethical responsibility to respect the service user's right to self-determination and to regard family members as active rather than passive recipients of services, they provide an effective framework for planning in partnership.

Exercise 8.3: Agreeing the Plan

TASKS:

1. Prepare a draft agreement detailing the plans that you have been making for accommodating Alison and Michael.

2. Identify the areas of negotiation required.

Points to Consider

1. Have you identified those parts of the written agreement that are non-negotiable (e.g. statutory requirements)?

2. Is the agreement written in such a way that the children will understand it?

3. Will the children be asked to sign it? Who will advise them on the content of the agreement?

4. Does the agreement include the foster carers? If not, why not?

5. Have you made provision for review and possible revision of the agreement?

6. Are the tasks that fall to you and your agency made as explicit as they can be?

CONCLUSION

In his book, *Introduction to Social Work Theory*, David Howe (1987), reviews the literature that describes what the users of social work services perceive as effective help. He is in no doubt that service users often feel confused, threatened and angered by the social worker who is vague or uncertain about their role and purpose:

> Both social workers and clients should know where they are and where they would like to go. If you do not know where you are, you will not know in which direction to move. If you do not know where you are going, you will not know when you have arrived. Drift and a lack of purpose in much social work practice suggests that many social workers have little idea of place in their work with clients. Thus a sense of location and a sense of direction should structure practice. (p.6)

If you are to prevent you and the children and families becoming lost in the wood like poor Alice, never venture far without a plan of where it is you are seeking to go.

NOTES AND SELF-ASSESSMENT

1. Do you think that social work really is about 'making things happen'?

2. Do you think that planning of the sort described in this Unit might rob social work of its creativity and spontaneity?

3. How 'planned' would you say your life is? What might this suggest about your attitude to planning?

4. Do you believe that, in the 'real world', planning in any kind of detail would prove impossible? What would be the consequences of not planning?

5. Given the statutory basis of much social work in this area, how free
    to plan are you?

6. How good are you at 'sticking' to a plan?

RECOMMENDED READING

Bryer, M. (1988) *Planning in Child Care.* London: BAAF.
DOH (1994) *Planning Long Term Placements Study.* London: HMSO.
Aldgate, J. (ed) (1989) *Using Written Agreements with Children and Families.*
    London: FRG.

TRAINER'S NOTES

Exercise 8.1: Goal Setting

A larger group can be subdivided with two groups asked to plan on behalf
of each child separately and a third on behalf of both children together.
Subsequent discussion should be aimed at reconciling any differences.
Once agreed, it is helpful to ask participants to role play presenting the
plan in summarised form (i.e. 'bullet points'), either for the purpose of a
simulated case conference or for discussion with the children and parents
concerned. It is a useful corrective for over-ambitious plans if the Trainer
consistently asks participants *how* they will achieve what is being proposed
as well as *when.*

Exercise 8.2: Planning For Placement

For the purposes of tasks 2 and 3, a larger group can be subdivided in
order to provide a contrast between ideal solutions (i.e. unlimited time, no
bureaucratic hurdles, etc.) and the practical task of planning in practice.
Discussion should focus on the acceptability of the compromises that will
have to be made. Task 4 can be undertaken by one group with access to

the Regulations and by another without. This provides an opportunity to evaluate what the Act requires and what the various parties to the process might ideally want.

Exercise 8.3: Agreeing the Plan

A larger group can begin by 'quickthinking' all of the areas that such an agreement should cover. Smaller groups can then draw up the details of the agreement and present them to an 'ethics committee' of the whole group which will evaluate the agreement in terms of its tone much more than its content. The group should re-read Study Text 4.3 before establishing its own evaluative criteria.

UNIT 9
Child Protection

OBJECTIVES

In this unit you will:

- Explore aspects of awareness and recognition of child abuse.
- Explore aspects of risk assessment in child protection.
- Explore the investigative process as defined by the Children Act 1989.
- Learn how child protection services and systems are organised and administered.

 **SOME BASICS**

In Unit 6 we explored how the term 'child abuse' and the realities it describes are socially constructed and, in part, subjectively defined. The same can be said for 'child protection'. Consider, for example, how a distinction might be made between being 'protected' and feeling 'safe' (Butler and Williamson 1994). 'Safe' is a word that some young people use to describe someone who can be trusted, who actively listens to what they are being told and who shows respect for the young person's feelings, their judgement and their right to confidentiality. 'Protected' can imply the mechanistic operation of the various bureaucratic arrangements, legal processes and social work strategies that adults impose upon young people when they have been, or are likely to be, harmed by another adult. Our present point is not just that 'child protection' can be understood differently depending, for example, on your relationship to the 'facts' of the case but that there is a qualitative dimension to child protection practice just as there is to social work practice with children and families in any other context. The experience of being 'protected' can be made better or worse by the manner in which it is achieved.

The point has, perhaps, best, and most famously, been made by Lord Justice Butler-Sloss in her report of the events in Cleveland. Butler-Sloss LJ noted, after criticising some aspects of professional practice undertaken as part of a child protection intervention, that a 'child is a person and not just an object of concern' (Cleveland Report 1988). A child's longer term interests, dignity and sense of identity, already made vulnerable by the process of abuse, must be preserved through any process of child 'protection'. The investigation of abuse, for example, can, without proper regard for the rights of the child and the alleged perpetrator, itself become abusive – as events in Orkney and Cleveland have been held to demonstrate (see Unit 5). As such, child protection practice must be firmly embedded in the context of attitudes, values and best practice in other areas of social work with children and families. Child protection is a *specialist* field but it is not to be understood as a *separate* field of practice.

Hence, this Unit, whilst focusing on child protection processes and practice, will do so in the context of knowledge, skills and values that have a more general application. We have chosen to do this not only because it would be absurd to try and compress a comprehensive account of practice in child protection into a single chapter but also because we believe that there are dangers if social workers and other professionals think about child protection in terms which isolate it from a broader understanding of what social work with children and families means. In working through this Unit, therefore, we do not want you to jettison all that you have thought about in terms of attitudes, values and the essentials of good practice just because you are engaged in 'child protection'. We cannot take you far into an understanding of the complexities of practice in this area (we purposely omit any reference to post-abuse work as this is well beyond the scope of a book such as this) but we do want you to begin your journey with a positive regard for what you know rather than with misgivings about what you have yet to learn.

For example, you will have considered, as part of Units 4 and 5, the local authority's general duty to 'safeguard and promote' the welfare of children (see CA 1989, s.17(1) and s.22(3)). This duty should govern your understanding of work to protect children from harm just as much as it should your work in supporting children and families in other circumstances. You are required to 'safeguard' the welfare of the child – which might imply the sense usually associated with the term 'protect' – but, at the same time, you are required to 'promote' his or her welfare. Neither, on its own, is sufficient. The following exercise, based on developments with the Taylor family, should demonstrate to you what you already know about 'protecting' children.

Taylor Family Case File

Despite the careful arrangements that you made for the children, you have had to revise your plans once again. Ron could not bring himself to consent to Alison and Michael being provided with accommodation and decided to exercise his parental responsibility and make arrangements of his own. With Tracy's blessing, and with the informed consent of both Alison and Michael, the older children have gone to live with Ron and his wife and child in Northtown. Supervision by the local social services department has been arranged and you have been invited to monthly review meetings with the children, Ron and the area social worker. The children are to have unrestricted contact with Tracy.

All of this has happened very quickly and the children moved to Northtown on the 19th February. Tracy and John continued to live at Mrs Taylor's (Senior) house on Old Estate. At first everything seemed to be going along well: the older children had settled down in Northtown and were making good progress in school and at home and Tracy seemed to be getting on well with her mother. Tracy said that she didn't really need your help and your visits declined to no more than once every three weeks.

In early May the local health visitor telephoned to say that she had recently seen John at the GP's request. The GP had noted that John was being brought to the surgery very frequently with a succession of minor childhood ailments. The GP indicated that she thought John 'wasn't being very well cared for' and that 'he looked a bit on the thin side'. You visited the home on the 14th of May. The house was dirty and very disorganised. Tracy told you that John was 'off his food and had the runs'. When asked about the state of the house, Tracy said that Alun had started to call around and was being very difficult and that the stress she was feeling meant that she had 'let things slide a bit'. Her mother, according to Tracy, 'couldn't be bothered', leaving more for her to do than she could manage. There had been a minor fire in the kitchen recently which made matters look worse than they were, according to Tracy. You arranged for the repair of the kitchen via the local authority's maintenance department and for the temporary re-connection of the gas supply, which had been turned off four months ago because of unpaid bills. You also arranged for a cash payment (via CA 1989, s.17(6)) to enable Tracy to stock up with food. Tracy agreed to attend the local Child Health Clinic on a weekly basis and accepted your offer of referral to the local Family Centre where John could attend 'toddlers club' and Tracy could meet other women in her position who might be able to offer advice and support.

On the 3rd of June the health visitor informed you that Tracy had not kept a single appointment at the Clinic. On the same day that the Health Visitor had been in touch, Tracy turned up at your office (while you were out) and left a message to say that she wasn't getting on with the Health Visitor and asking that you visit her. You tried, on four occasions over the next three weeks, to see Tracy but she was never in at the times at which you had agreed to call. On the last day of June, during evening surgery, Tracy called at the Clinic to see the Health Visitor. The Health Visitor had left for the day but Tracy was seen briefly by the Practice Nurse who said she would pass on a message to the Health Visitor in the morning. There has been no response, as yet, from the Family Centre to which you had referred Tracy.

In the first week of July an anonymous caller informs your duty office that a young child had been left unattended in the garden for most of the day. He was crying and there didn't seem to be anyone looking after him. The address given was Mrs Taylor's house in Old Estate. You visit and find Tracy at home. You tell her what you have been told. Tracy explains that she has been away for a few days with Alun and that her mother was supposed to be looking after John. Tracy tells you that Mrs Taylor (Senior) has taken John out in his buggy. They both return while you are still there. John is still clearly very distressed. Mrs Taylor explains that 'he must have caught the sun' and that he's just 'hot and bothered'. Tracy accuses her mother of not looking after John. She responds that Tracy shouldn't have gone off and left him like she did and an argument between the two begins to develop. Each accuses the other of failing to look after John properly. Tracy shouts at John that this wouldn't have happened if it wasn't for him.

John is sitting silently in his buggy, watching what is going on around him. You intervene in the argument between the two women. You observe that John is sitting in a very dirty nappy and that his buggy is filthy and very smelly. Neither Tracy nor Mrs Taylor seem prepared to do anything about this. Tracy says that she will see to John after you've gone. You notice that he has a number of what appear to be bruises on his arms with two much darker ones on each arm, just below the shoulder. You ask Tracy how he got them and she explains that Alun had been playing 'aeroplanes' with him. Mrs Taylor (Senior) asks Tracy whether Alun had been around the house as she never wanted to see him again. Tracy says that she hadn't seen Alun and it was the boyfriend of a friend of her's who had been playing with John. You ask Tracy to meet you at the Clinic in the morning. She doesn't keep her appointment but does see the duty doctor later in the day. The doctor is clear that John is underweight for his age and that he is suffering from moderate sunburn and impetigo, aggravated by urine burns. He insists that you visit and 'get this sorted out'.

 ### Exercise 9.1 Safeguarding and Promoting

Having read the account of developments in the Taylor family, complete the following tasks. Today is 3 August.

1. Write down what you consider to be John's primary needs at this point.

2. Identify exactly how you might verify your assessment of John's needs.

3. Assuming that John's needs are as you predicted, identify the ways in which these might be met.

4. How far does your answer to (3) adequately safeguard and promote John's welfare?

Points to Consider

1. Which of John's needs must be met in order to 'safeguard' his welfare?

2. Which of John's needs must be met in order to 'promote' his welfare?

3. Write short definitions of what you understand by the terms 'safeguard' and 'promote', in order to clarify their meaning for you.

4. Do you consider John to be an abused child? If so, at what point did this case become a 'child protection' one? Be clear about your reasons.

5. Would such a determination make you revise your plans for investigating John's situation further?

6. Would such a determination make you want to revise your plans for meeting John's needs?

RECOGNISING CHILD ABUSE

It might reasonably be argued that all of the work undertaken so far with the Taylor family is aimed at child protection, in its very broadest sense, in so far as it was intended to 'safeguard and promote' the children's welfare. John's situation is now (probably) an abusive one, however, and your answers to the questions posed by the last Exercise, and to the points that you have been asked to consider, should have raised new and more pressing concerns for you. John almost certainly needs a more immediate and direct form of protection now. Even so, in safeguarding John's welfare from this point on, it will be vital to ensure that we continue to consciously and actively promote it too.

As suggested in Unit 6, child abuse rarely presents itself in a dramatic or easily identifiable form. Families where child abuse occurs may not be immediately distinctive from other families with which you are working.

Sometimes, especially in the case of neglect, what has been a chronic family situation, such as that described in the Taylor file, may shift catastrophically into some other more easily-defined form of abuse. Indeed, in Unit 10, we will see that this is what happens in this case. But, at this stage we will clearly need to investigate John's situation further. We will need to have regard to what predictive and diagnostic indicators of abuse are present and to evaluate the degree of current and potential risk to John. The following Study Text will describe some of the more frequently used diagnostic indicators that may inform your recognition of abuse.

Study Text 9.1: Recognising Child Abuse

For present purposes, we will be using a more limited categorisation of abuse than that which we used in Unit 6. It is that used by social services departments for recording entries in the child protection register (see Study Text 9.3) and by the Department of Health for statistical purposes. It is taken from *Working Together Under the Children Act* (DOH 1991g), an important source of guidance for work in this field.

The definitions of abuse offered in *Working Together* (pp.48–9) are:

- *Neglect*: The persistent or severe neglect of a child, or the failure to protect a child from exposure to any kind of danger, including cold or starvation, or extreme failure to carry out important aspects of care, resulting in the significant impairment of the child's health or development, including non-organic failure to thrive.

- *Physical Injury*: Actual or likely physical injury to a child, or failure to prevent physical injury (or suffering) to a child including deliberate poisoning, suffocation and Munchausen's syndrome by proxy.

- *Sexual Abuse*: Actual or likely sexual exploitation of a child or adolescent. The child may be dependent and/or developmentally immature.

- *Emotional Abuse.* Actual or likely severe adverse effect on the emotional and behavioural development of a child caused by persistent or severe emotional ill-treatment or rejection. All abuse involves some emotional ill-treatment.

In this Study Text we have chosen to concentrate on neglect. We do so because it is one of the most difficult forms of abuse to detect and because of our belief that social workers, and others, have the greatest difficulty in recognising and responding to neglect. We will deal with emotional abuse in the context of other forms of abuse.

NEGLECT

Using NSPCC registers for the period 1977 – 1986, Creighton (1986) has shown that children who suffer neglect or emotional abuse have consistently been registered in comparatively small numbers. However, the relationship between child abuse registers and the actual incidence of child abuse is problematic and the relatively low rate of registration of such cases may have more to do with social workers' difficulty in recognising these forms of abuse and their reluctance to respond rather than the frequency of the event itself.

Difficulty in recognition has to be understood against the background of the very broad range of a child's emotional, psychological and physical needs, many of which are age specific. Accordingly, universally reliable indicators of neglect are as elusive as any comprehensive definition of the process itself. Moreover, neglect is about things undone rather than things done, acts of omission rather than commission and non-events are that much more difficult to observe, of course. Also, neglect, by definition, occurs over a period of time and may proceed almost imperceptibly.

Neglect can only be identified by comparison with the circumstances and development of the non-neglected child. In terms of general development, particularly in the case of infants and children under five, there are recognised standards against which any individual's progress or lack of it can be measured. Where a child's general development is delayed other than for medical reasons (non-organic failure to thrive), although usually the province of the health visitor, the social worker still has an important role to play. You should be concerned if a young child suffers repeatedly from chronic diarrhoea, recurrent and persistent infections, voracious appetite or no appetite at all, a child who thrives whilst away from home and/or a general delay in acquiring such skills as sitting, crawling, walking and talking.

In behavioural terms, a neglected or emotionally abused child may be unresponsive to social stimulation and avoid eye contact. They may also exhibit excessively 'clingy' behaviour developed through lack of confidence and any sense of emotional or physical security. There may be signs of self-stimulating behaviour, such as head-banging or rocking. Most striking of all (and not confined to neglect or emotional abuse) is the child who distances himself from others and observes whatever is happening in an attitude of 'frozen watchfulness', ready to respond to a blow or a threat but not actively engaged with what is going on around them.

The older child may appear more obviously dirty and unkempt. They may be smelly and dirty. They may rush around, unable to concentrate on anything for very long and may have great difficulty in playing with other children. They may also be 'touch hungry' and seek physical contact, even from strangers. There may be additional signs of self-stimulating behaviour, including self-harm. At school there may be apparent signs of learning difficulties and poor peer relationships as well as social and emotional immaturity.

Whilst neglect is a difficult area, both conceptually and definitionally, this is not the most important consideration in relation to child protection practice and the neglect of children. Research has shown (Reder, Duncan and Gray 1993; Minty and Patterson 1994) that our collective tolerance of the neglect of children is far too high and that the comparative neglect of neglected children by those professionals who's job it is to protect them needs to be carefully examined.

It is possible to suggest a number of explanations for the failure to see abuse, even if signs of the neglect are obvious:

- In our work generally, and in child protection specifically, we are too much concerned with the actions and behaviour of adults and too little concerned with the consequences for children. Few of us would tolerate a urine soaked mattress, infestation or prolonged cold and hunger for ourselves or those close to us for a moment longer than we could avoid, yet child death enquiries would seem to indicate that we will accept excuses from adults for the neglectful treatment of some children.

- We avoid confronting neglect through misplaced cultural relativism. We console ourselves with the thought that 'Children around here all live like that. They may be scruffy, but they're happy!' *All* children have a right to adequate standards of care and a right to our protection.

- We confuse neglect with poverty. It is true that, in the context of structural poverty, the potential for children to lead impoverished lives on a grand scale is disturbingly high. The fact of structural economic inequality and the consequences of poverty provide a bleak background against which to identify particular instances of neglect. But, it is a dangerous fallacy to locate the responsibility for neglect other than with a child's carers. Responsibility is not, of course, the same as blame. Minty and Patterson (1994) writing about neglect, are clear that poverty increases the likelihood of neglect and that living in poverty increases the likelihood of being officially labelled as neglectful; poverty attracts the attention of the authorities as parents are forced to ask for financial or other assistance; poverty forces cruel choices on parents and increases the stress of parenting, etc. But, many children and their parents achieve 'good enough' parenting despite the grinding poverty that is the lot of so many parents and children today.

- Linked with this idea is also the 'Fear of the Flood': this is the very real anxiety that were anyone to move the current threshold of tolerance of neglect, personally and organisationally, we would be overwhelmed.

- We also avoid neglect through falling in with the general sense of hopelessness that can infuse such cases. This sense of hopelessness arises because of the elusive nature of much neglect which often leaves the social worker with no specific behaviour or clear circumstances to work with to bring about change. Indeed, long-term interventions may seem wholly unproductive as they attempt to address the personalities of the carers or else rely inappropriately on 'support services' which maintain, rather than reduce, the problem. In other words, neglect cases can seem deeply unsatisfying in professional terms and their hopelessness can easily become ours.

PHYSICAL ABUSE

Distinguishing between a non-accidental injury and an accidental one is no more straightforward than being able to identify neglect, even for skilled forensic paediatricians. All children collect bruises and other signs of injury as part of the routine business of being a child and, although there are patterns of difference between accidental and non-accidental

Sign of Injury	Non-accidental	Accidental
Bruise:	more numerous; bruises may be at different stages of healing; often found in soft tissue, e.g. ear, cheeks, mouth; often patterned, e.g. finger and thumb pinch mark, slap mark or imprint of hard object; may be symmetrical, e.g. grab marks on both arms or ears, two black eyes	likely to be few and scattered; likely to occur where bone is close to surface, e.g. forehead, elbow, knee or shins
Burns:	contact burn likely to show distinct boundary, e.g. hot-plate, cigarette burn; likely to be at unusual site, e.g. palm of hand, top of thigh, buttocks.	likely to be treated, easily explained and minor, e.g. brush with cigarette rather than defined edge
Fractures:	numerous and not appropriate to age and stage; may include ribs or skull; 'spiral' fractures	likely to be arms and legs; fractures are rare in babies and young children
Other Injuries:	large bites, fingernail marks, deep cuts, poisoning	minor and superficial likely to have been treated

Figure 9.1: Indicators of physical abuse

injuries, there are exceptions to almost every rule. The typology in Figure 9.1 is typical of many that you will come across.

Remember that as well as the physiological signs of physical abuse, the child may also show similar social, emotional and psychological attributes to those described as consequent upon neglect. Remember also that every one of those indicators associated with non-accidental injury can have an accidental cause.

SEXUAL ABUSE

There are a number of physical signs that may be associated with sexual abuse. These are not usually accessible to the social worker and need careful consideration by a paediatrician. They include injury to genital area (these are often minor but inconsistent with accidental injury), vaginal or anal soreness, discharge or bleeding, presence of a sexually transmitted disease, soft tissue injury to breast, buttocks or thighs, love bites and semen stains and/or pubic hair on skin or clothes.

The social worker is more likely to be alerted to sexual abuse through the behaviour of the child. The interpretation of behaviour is a notoriously imprecise science and the investigation of sexual abuse remains a highly contested area – it is also one that is much better left to more experienced practitioners than those we imagine might read this book. However, there are some indicators that are more useful than others and which may alert you to the need to report any concerns that you may have to others better placed to investigate and evaluate them – these include a preoccupation with sexual matters and compulsive sexual behaviour. Most children are curious about sexual matters but overtly sexualised behaviour, attempts at simulating sexual acts, persistent masturbation in public or anatomically detailed drawings by younger children should be taken as causes for concern.

In older and younger children the stigma and sense of betrayal associated with sexual abuse can produce profound psychological effects, which may manifest themselves in severe depression, self-harm, suicide attempts and severe social isolation. Self-evidently, these indicators, what-ever their cause, should be a cause of concern to every social worker.

RECOGNISING ABUSE

At several points we have indicated that almost each and every sign of abuse can have an innocent explanation. Certain medical conditions can produce bruising, skin disclourations and fractures. The most unlikely accidents do happen. None of the indicators, taken in isolation, can ever be considered as conclusive evidence of abuse. Nonetheless, it is important to recognise that the absence of proof in child abuse is not proof of absence (Sgroi 1982) and you must always give serious thought and proper consideration to any and every indication of possible abuse.

In particular, your concern should be heightened in those situations where there has been a failure or reluctance to seek appropriate medical advice or assistance, where the account of the injury or other indication is not credible in terms of the child's age and stage of development or where the account changes when closely examined or when carers give inconsistent accounts of the same series of events.

However, the essential uncertainty which remains at the heart of child protection practice need not lead you to over-predict abuse or to fail to recognise it when it is happening. Whether your strategy is an optimistic one (which rushes to find or accept innocent explanations for indications of abuse), whether it is a pessimistic one (which finds evidence of abuse in innocent, if unfortunate, circumstances) (Dingwall 1989) or whether it is a balanced one will be a function of how acute are your observations, how extensive and current is your knowledge base and how far you have consciously developed the capacity to exercise your professional judgement. It is only through the exercise of that judgement that the determination of abuse can be made.

Exercise 9.2: Signs of Neglect

Read over the case notes for the Taylor family in this Unit and in Units 7 and 8 and then:

1. Write down those indicators of the possible abuse and/or neglect of John that you find in the case notes.

2. Try and construct a completely innocent explanation for each of the indicators you have listed at (1).

3. Make a list of the additional information you might need to verify or reject your suspicions of neglect and/or other forms of abuse.

Points to Consider

1. How confident do you feel now about whether John is being abused?

2. How much additional information would be required to convince you?

3. How confident would you need to feel before you decided that matters should be further investigated or action taken?

4. Do you think that, in the circumstances, what is happening to John was probably inevitable and, as such, unavoidable?

5. Who is responsible for the standard of John's care?

6. What might prevent you from seeing evidence of neglect or other forms of abuse?

 **RISK**

There are few incontrovertible indicators of abuse and no checklists or simple measures that you can apply to establish the facts easily. But, the forensic determination of the 'facts' of abuse is only one dimension to the process. There is also the determination of risk.

Questions of risk are of particular and acute interest to many social scientists today. They recognise that we are all becoming more aware of, and averse to, risk. Evidence of this can be found, for example, in the development of systems for the careful, hi-tech monitoring of the health of mother and child through pregnancy, which has produced dramatic falls in the rate of infant and maternal mortality since the War. At the same time, these very techno-economic developments make us all more risk prone. The consequences of one major nuclear accident would have a much greater effect on generations of children yet unborn than any progress we might have made in perinatal care over recent years. Consequently, as well as creating risk through social, cultural and technological processes, society is actively engaged in weighing up the potential social benefits of any risk against the potential social costs. In our own field, for example, the social and economic costs of the kind of surveillance that could *guarantee* the protection of children has to be weighed against the social costs of gross interference by the state with the 'sanctity of the domestic hearth'. The following Study Text explores risk in the context of child protection.

Study Text 9.2: Risk Evaluation

There is a wide diversity of expert approaches to risk. Engineers, economists and actuaries attempt to predict the probability of hazardous events, such as natural disasters. Lawyers and criminologists have examined the control and regulation of behaviour that serves the maintenance and order of society. Psychologists and sociologists have explored a variety of forms of risk behaviour, including sexual promiscuity and drug misuse. From this diversity of approaches, an important definitional distinction emerges: that between risk and risk evaluation.

Risk has been defined as: 'the probability that a particular adverse event occurs during a stated period of time, or results from a particular challenge' and risk evaluation as: 'the complex process of determining the significance or value of the identified hazards and estimated risks to those concerned with or affected by the decision' (Royal Society 1992).

Risk is a matter of statistical calculation; risk evaluation is a matter of subjective judgement, and the two do not necessarily coincide. For example, researchers in the US (Fischoff *et al.* 1981) determined the risk of death from various causes. A large sample of the general public was then told the number of deaths arising from road accidents and asked to estimate the numbers of deaths from other specified causes. Not surprisingly, vivid deaths, such as those arising from botulism or tornados, were overestimated and those arising from less dramatic causes, such as cancer or a stroke, were underestimated. Clearly, the statistical likelihood of an event occurring and the subjective estimation of that event occurring can vary. This Study Text will explore risk in child protection by considering what we know about risk calculation and what practitioners can do to optimise the conditions in which to carry out the subjective process of risk evaluation.

RISK CALCULATION

Not all risks can be calculated to precise actuarial standards. Many hazards are cumulative, diffuse, slow acting and insidious. They have diverse causes and complex mechanisms. There is uncertainty about the nature, scale and timing of possible outcomes and the cost of error in policy and personal terms can be high. Child abuse is one such 'elusive hazard' (Kates 1985). Yet, in child protection practice there have emerged, at different times and according to particular ways of understanding abuse, several types of risk assessment instruments aimed at identifying when a child is at risk or is likely to be so in the future

These risk assessment instruments are usually produced in the forms of check-lists. A particularly well-known one is that produced by Greenland in 1987 and referred to in Reder, Duncan and Gray's (1993) influential book on the non-accidental deaths of children, *Beyond Blame – Child Abuse Tragedies Revisited.* Greenland describes risk factors associated with the parents of a child at risk and those of the child itself (Figure 9.2).

But, despite being well established, Greenland's check-list can be criticised as much for what it omits as for what it includes. For example, as Reder points out, Greenland's check-list does not include the frustration of access to a child as a warning sign, although Greenland's own work would suggest that it is a significant risk indicator. Nor does it recognise how crises elsewhere in the family's life or relationships between parents/partners heighten the risk to the child. From Reder's work other risk indicators were identified, which included the failure of children to live up to the role expectations carers had for them. The period following a return home from care was particularly dangerous in this respect.

Parent

Was previously abused/neglected as a child

Has a history of abusive/neglectful parenting

Has a history of criminal assaultive and/or suicidal behaviour

Is a single parent, separated or the partner is not the biological parent

Is socially isolated, including frequent moves and poor housing

Is poor, unemployed, an unskilled worker or received inadequate education

Abuses alcohol or drugs

Is pregnant or in the post-partum period or has a chronic illness

Child

Was previously abused/neglected, especially when under five years of age

Was premature or of low birthweight

Has a birth defect, a chronic illness or developmental lag

Had prolonged separation from the mother

Is adopted, fostered or a step child

Is currently underweight

Cries frequently or is difficult to comfort

Shows difficulties in feeding or elimination

Figure 9.2 Greenland's check-list

However, the most significant indicator of danger to the child, identified by Reder, and illustrated in the Taylor case, was what he termed 'closure' in the family-professional interaction. Closure manifested itself in families actively reducing contact with the outside world, with few people able to meet or speak with them. Curtains would be kept drawn, children would not play outside or attend nursery, appointments and meetings were missed, etc. The same effect can also be achieved through flight (where parents/carers move from their accommodation) or disguised compliance (where parents appeared to be co-operating with the plans made but rarely actually did) or by popping up in unexpected places, with the effect that suspicion or concern is lowered – that is turning up at the health visitors but not at the case review.

The point to be made is that such check-lists, and any commentaries upon them, at best describe broad sets of circumstances that are associated with child abuse. They rarely, if ever, approach being able to give causal accounts or even strong correlations. In fact, almost all of the research that informs the determination of such risk factors is methodologically very weak. As has been pointed out elsewhere (Dingwall 1989), these studies are often based on non-representative samples, are retrospective, demonstrate associations rather than causal links or directions or use broad definitions of child abuse.

Even if one was persuaded not to dwell on the technical deficiencies of the research that informs these risk assessment instruments, in practice, such assessment tools have proved generally unhelpful. A particular problem that many of them share is the production of false positives (predicting abuse which then does not occur) and false negatives (failing to predict abuse that does then occur) (Dingwall 1989). We might note Reder's conclusion that the abuse of children can neither be 'confidently predicted or completely prevented'.

Notwithstanding this, child protection takes place as a professional activity, legitimated and, indeed, required by state and society and risk assessment still plays a major part in professional practice. Check-lists may prove more or less helpful to you as a way of guiding and structuring your assessment but the process remains one of applying general rules to specific situations and, as such, much more of an art than any kind of science. It remains an exercise in judgement still. This is a further illustration of the absolute requirement to embrace the necessary uncertainty that surrounds any form of risk assessment.

But, is there anything that can be done to improve our capacity to exercise that judgement more effectively?

IMPROVING RISK EVALUATION IN CHILD PROTECTION

The work of Maureen Stone (1992) begins from two basic premises derived from a review of risk assessment research in areas other than child protection. First, that the process of risk assessment and decision making must be an open one where, as far as is possible, the various influences on the person making the assessment are acknowledged and accorded appropriate significance. Second, as assessment and decision making are human activities, it is essential to consider the human element. In child protection this means being aware of the potential consequences for the practice of the personal and professional circumstances of the practitioner. Stone goes on to argue that the negative impact of particular circumstances in which the practitioner may be working – such as feeling inadequately supervised or supported, feeling burnt out, experiencing poor inter-agency relationships, working in an organisation which is undergoing unsettling change or feeling highly under-resourced – can add to the level of risk a child faces through indirect means, namely through having an influence on the type of decisions and responses taken by that practitioner.

The model of risk assessment that she develops, as well as taking into account primary risk factors relating to the child and its family and the social, financial and environmental context in which it lives, also takes account of secondary risk factors which are related to the context in which the risk assessment takes place. These include (p.26):

- the nature of the child protection organisation (e.g. its structure and management and the quality of staff support and supervision)

- human failings (e.g. poor relationships, tiredness and stress)

- deficits and resource problems (e.g. training deficits, poor recording or other skills)

- inter-agency problems (e.g. different professional values, communication difficulties)

- media pressure/fear of ridicule (e.g. 'defensive social work', doing only what is uncontroversial).

The following exercise should help you explore the context of decision making in your own agency.

Exercise 9.3: Risk Evaluation

Using Stone's classification of secondary risk factors, undertake an 'audit' of the decision making context of the particular work setting or practice placement in which you are located. You should ensure that you can answer at least the following questions:

1. Your own organisation:
   - Are lines of accountability clear?
   - Are the support services adequate?

- Are records easy to find?
- How long does it take for case notes to be updated?
- Do you have time to think as well as act?

2. Human failings:

- Do you have strategies for dealing with stress?
- Do you have the skills needed to do your job properly?
- Do you have strong feelings about the people you work with/for?

3. Deficits and resource problems:

- Can you see the children and families with whom you are working sufficiently often?
- Are the available material and human resources required by your work sufficient?
- Who provides leadership in your work setting?

4. Inter-agency problems:

- Do you understand what the other agencies you regularly work with are really trying to do?
- How might you check your understanding of other agencies' priorities?
- Do you think that partner agencies understand what your agency is trying to achieve?

5. Media pressure/fear of ridicule:

- Are there recommendations that you would not dare make in reports?
- Are there people in your organisation whom you would never contradict or challenge?
- Are case notes written up with a public inquiry or the editor of the local paper in mind?

Points to Consider

1. In your view, how far do these 'secondary risk' factors influence the quality of risk assessment in your agency?

2. Do you think that your colleagues are aware of the potential effect of such factors?

3. How can you make them more aware?

4. What can you do to reduce the impact of any one of these factors on your own, and your agency's, capacity to evaluate risk?

5. How might your colleagues react to your questioning of risk assessment processes in your agency?

6. How safe is risk evaluation in your agency?

SOME LIMITATIONS

It is beyond the scope of this book to simulate a credible organisational context and culture for you to explore further, although you are encouraged to pursue some of these issues through the reading that has been recommended at the end of this Unit. In terms of the Taylor family, we have determined that some further investigation is necessary. The following Study Text explores how the Children Act 1989 and *Working Together* inform that investigative process and establish the structure that will decide what happens next.

Study Text 9.3: Investigation, Decision Making and Review

THE AREA CHILD PROTECTION COMMITTEE

The precise details of the investigative process in any particular local authority area will be part of a published set of Child Protection Procedures. These procedures will have been discussed and agreed by the several agencies involved in child protection in that area. Those agencies will almost always include the social services department, the police, staff of the health service (including Primary and Community Health Services and Family Health Service Authorities), the probation service and the education service. These agencies, and possibly others – such as the NSPCC, will be members of the Area Child Protection Committee (ACPC). The main tasks of the ACPC are set out in *Working Together Under the Children Act 1989* (DOH 1991g, para. 2.12 [and 8.1]):

- to establish, maintain and review local inter-agency guidelines on procedures to be followed in individual cases
- to monitor the implementation of legal procedures
- to identify significant issues arising from the handling of cases and reports from inquiries
- to scrutinise arrangements to provide treatment, expert advice and inter-agency liaison and make recommendations to the responsible agencies
- to scrutinise progress on work to prevent child abuse and make recommendations to the responsible agencies
- to scrutinise work related to inter-agency training and make recommendations to the responsible agencies
- to conduct reviews (in the case of the death of a child or where a child protection issue arises of major public concern)
- to publish an annual report about local child protection matters.

Given that each area will have interpreted the requirements of *Working Together* differently to reflect local needs and service structures, it is of the utmost importance that you familiarise yourself with the procedures determined by the appropriate ACPC for the area in which you work and make yourself fully conversant with the responsibilities attaching to your agency and your post. The remainder of this Study Text can only provide a schematic account of the investigative and decision making structures as established by the Children Act 1989 (the Act) and *Working Together*, which does not relieve you of your professional responsibility to read and fully understand your own local procedures and your role within them.

THE INVESTIGATIVE PROCESS

The local authority has a statutory duty under s.47 of the Act to investigate whenever it 'has reasonable cause to believe that a child who lives, or is found, in their area is suffering, or is likely to suffer significant harm' (s.47 (1)(b)) (see Study Text 10.1 for a full definition of 'significant harm'). The primary aims of the investigation are to:

- establish the facts and the circumstances giving rise to the concern
- decide if there are grounds for concern
- to identify sources and level of risk
- decide protective or other action in relation to the child and others.

   (DOH 1991g, para. 4.14.3)

Specifically, the Act requires the local authority to determine whether it should apply to the court for an order or exercise any of its powers under the Act, including the provision of services to the child and its family. In order to assist in this determination, section 47 requires the local authority to take 'such steps as are reasonably practical' (s.47 (4)) to obtain access to the child, either directly or through a person authorised by the authority 'unless they are satisfied that they already have sufficient information with respect to [the child]'. If access is frustrated, the local authority must apply to the court for one of a range of orders (see Unit 10) unless it is satisfied that the child's welfare can be 'satisfactorily safeguard without their doing so' (s.47 (6)). In the course of its investigations under s.47 the local authority can make reasonable requests for information from any local authority, including education and housing authorities. At the end of the investigation, the local authority must take such action as it decides is appropriate. If the decision is not to apply to the court for an order, the local authority should consider whether it would be appropriate to review the case at a later date.

Working Together (para.5.13) recommends that at the commencement of the investigative process there should be a strategy discussion between the statutory agencies involved in order to plan and co-ordinate the investigation and to clarify the roles of the various agencies. This discussion may not necessarily involve a meeting.

THE INITIAL CASE CONFERENCE

Between 8 and 15 working days after the start of the investigation, as determined by the local child protection procedures as well as the particular circumstances of the child, an initial child protection case conference should be called. Local procedures will determine the arrangements for the chairing of case conferences and the provision of support services, including the taking of minutes.

The purpose of the case conference is to bring together the family and the professionals involved and provide them 'with the opportunity to exchange information and plan together' (DOH 1991g, para.6.1). The case conference does not need to make a determination that a particular person has committed the abuse. That is a matter for the courts. In fact: 'The only decision to be taken at the conference is whether or not to register the child and if, registration is agreed, to allocate the keyworker' (DOH 1991g, para. 5.15.4).

THE CHILD PROTECTION REGISTER

In each local authority area a child protection register must be maintained. 'This is not a register of children who have been abused but of children for whom there are currently unresolved child protection issues and for whom there is an inter-agency protection plan' (DOH 1991g, para. 6.36).

Children may be placed on the register in one of the various categories (described in Study Text 9.1) if the child protection case conference decides that one or more incidents 'which can be described as having adversely affected the child' have occurred or are likely to occur or that significant harm is expected on the 'basis of professional judgement of findings of the investigation in this individual case or on research evidence' (DOH 1991g, para.6.39). The register provides a mechanism for ensuring the regular review of children for whom there is an inter-agency plan, a speedy point of access to information for professionals who have concerns about a child and useful information for the ACPC and its members on patterns and trends in child protection practice.

THE KEYWORKER

The keyworker appointed, if a decision to register a child is made, must be a social worker from either the social services department or the NSPCC. Their role is to act as a focal point for the exchange of information and the maintenance of the inter-agency plan and to act as lead worker for their particular agency. The plan itself, which will usually begin with a comprehensive 'Orange Book' assessment (see Study Text 7. 2), must be recorded in writing. It should be reviewed regularly (usually every six months, or less, depending on the circumstances). The purpose of the review is to consider the arrangements in place to protect the child in the light of the current level of risk and to consider whether registration should be continued or not.

CONCLUSION

You must ensure that you have access to the child protection procedures for the area in which you work, or are on placement, at the earliest possible stage of your induction period. Unit 6 demonstrated how you may find yourself engaged in a child protection investigation long before you think you are ready. Your agency has a professional obligation to provide such access. You have a professional responsibility to make full use of it.

 ## CONCLUSION

Recognition of abuse, even in apparently 'clear cut' situations, must be preceded by an *awareness* on your part of the potential for abuse. We emphatically do *not* mean by this that every child and family case in which you are involved must be considered as a potential case of child abuse. What we mean is that if you do not have a clear sense of what is meant by 'good enough parenting', the needs and rights of children and a clear sense of your personal and professional thresholds, you might not be able to recognise abuse even when confronted with an unambiguous instance of it. The same point must be made in your considerations of an appropriate response. Both remain questions of professional judgement. That judgement can be informed by specialist knowledge and improved by the use of lessons learned by research but it must be predicated on a thorough grounding in the essentials of good practice.

We do not want you to feel intimidated by work in child protection. In this Unit you have already begun the process of making, testing and reflecting on your professional judgement in such cases, albeit only on paper. That judgement is rooted in your existing knowledge, skills and values. It is important to hold on to this thought, not just at the beginning of your career when it should give you confidence to extend your professional competence but also later in your career when familiarity with abuse can arouse no more than a weary cynicism.

NOTES AND SELF-ASSESSMENT

1. Do you want to work in child protection? Can you explain why/why not?
2. How prepared are you to work in child protection, in terms of knowledge and skills?
3. How prepared are you emotionally to work in this area?
4. What personal qualities could you bring to work in child protection?
5. Do you know what to do when you are confronted with an incident of possible abuse?
6. Where would you find the ACPC child protection procedures where you work?

RECOMMENDED READING

DOH (1995) *Child Protection – Messages from Research*. London: HMSO.
DOH (1991) *Working Together Under the Children Act 1989*. London: HMSO.
Gough, D. (1993) *Child Abuse Interventions – A Review of the Research Literature*. Glasgow: Public Health Research Unit, University of Glasgow.

TRAINER'S NOTES

Exercise 9.1: Safeguarding and Promoting

Tasks 1, 2 and 3 can be undertaken either in small groups or by 'quickthinking' in a larger group. Material generated can be organised according to the proto-assessment prepared as part of Exercise 7.3. It is important that Task 3 is not carried out with too much emphasis on what a local authority might *do* at this stage. The emphasis should be on John's needs. Ideas generated here can be reviewed in the light of participants' reading of Study Text 9.3 and compared to the range of options considered as part of Exercise 4.2.

Exercise 9.2: Signs of Neglect

This exercise is best conducted in pairs, with a plenary session to compare notes. Participants should be encouraged to let their imaginations operate freely at Task 2. The plausibility of each explanation can be tested in debate between its proponent(s) and the rest of the group. This usually demonstrates where individuals feature on the pessimistic/ optimistic continuum. The kind of information (i.e. doctor's assessments, teacher's observations, etc.) that may be suggested as part of Task 3 must include reference to the participant's own 'observations', notes, records and professional knowledge, etc. as there is sometimes a tendency for workers in child protection to look for 'proof' outside of their own knowledge and expertise.

Exercise 9.3: Risk Evaluation

Participants should be encouraged to prepare five minute presentations of their audit. Discussion should allow for comparisons to be made and for any patterns relating to an agency's capacity for safe decision making to emerge (e.g. size of organisation, management culture, etc.). The group should be encouraged to draw up an action plan or procedural guidance that they might be able to take back to their agency for further discussion.

UNIT 10

Going to Court

OBJECTIVES

In this unit you will:

- Rehearse the process for obtaining a Care Order.
- Learn how to prepare a witness statement.
- Explore some fundamentals of court craft.

 **GOING TO COURT**

The purpose of going to court is to obtain, vary or discharge an order in respect of a child. For many social workers, even the most experienced, going to court can seem a daunting prospect. We may feel uncertain at finding ourselves on unfamiliar territory where people around us dress differently, use a strange vocabulary and engage in rituals that we do not fully understand. Our apprehension may be increased by our awareness that a great deal depends on the outcome of the court hearing, not only for the child and family most immediately concerned but for us too. We may feel that our own reputation and self-esteem might be threatened, and even that justice might not be done, if we do not play our part fully.

A degree of apprehension, which appropriately reflects the seriousness of the occasion, is certainly preferable to a sense of complacency. If that apprehension provokes us to prepare assiduously and reflect seriously on the case before the court then it will have served a very useful purpose, for there can be no doubt that the court room can be a rigorous test of what we do and believe as social workers. We would probably agree that if our work could not bear close scrutiny then its deficiencies should be exposed. On the other hand, if it can withstand a thorough examination then we can proceed strengthened by the knowledge that our work has demonstrable rigour and coherence.

Just how early in your professional career or how frequently you will find yourself in court is very much more dependent on *where* you work than you might imagine. The highest rate of public law applications per 1000 of the population under 16 living in a local authority area is 26 times higher than the lowest. Even in neighbouring authorities where demographic variations are relatively minor, the rate of application to the courts can vary by a factor of eight (*Guardian 4/1/95*). Clearly, geography itself is not the issue, even taking into account broad economic and social differences between areas. The rate of applications to the court is in no small measure a function of local working practices and it remains the route into local authority care for the majority of young people (DOH 1996, p.6). This means that the kinds of decisions you and your colleagues make about whether or when to go to court and the outcomes you seek to achieve may be as important as the actual circumstances of children and families in determining the use made of compulsory powers.

This Unit aims to provide you with a practical appreciation of the process of going to court. Our particular interest in this Unit is in those public law orders that we may have to consider in relation to the Taylor Family and which you are more likely to encounter or make use of in practice. But, before we look in detail at what is involved in applying for a care order, we should catch up with events in the Taylor Family.

Taylor Family Case File

On the 3rd August you called at Mrs Taylor's (senior) house to see why Tracy had not turned up to meet you at the clinic as you had arranged, only to be told that Tracy had moved back in with Alun. Mrs Taylor told you that she and Tracy had had a major row over her various choices of partner. You were not able to visit Tracy in New Estate that day.

At lunchtime on the 4th August you received a telephone call from a very distraught Mrs Taylor (senior). She told you that Tracy had been to see her, with John, and that John had a very big bruise over his eye. Tracy had told her that Alun had hit John and Tracy. Mrs. Taylor had told Tracy that 'she had made her bed and so must lie in it' and to go home to Alun. She now very much regrets having said this and wants you to go and 'make sure that Tracy is all right'.

You arrived at Tracy's at around 2 pm. Upon arrival you found John playing in the front garden. He was digging a hole in the ground with a tin can. There was no gate on the garden, which fronts on to the busy main road. John was only wearing a T-shirt and nappy, despite the fact that it was drizzling and far from warm. There was no immediate sign of Tracy or Alun. As you picked John up you could feel how cold he was. You could also see what appeared to be bruises. There was a dark bruise over John's left eye and his right ear was red and swollen. There were also some yellow/brown marks on his neck; there were three on the left side of his neck and one on the right side. The one on the right side was bigger than the others, about the size of a 50p piece. There was a similar pattern of marks on John's left leg, above the knee; the larger mark was on the inside of his thigh. You took John into the house, the front door was open, and wrapped him in a towel that was lying in the hall at the foot of the stairs. You called out but received no answer.

On entering the front room you found Alun. He did not respond to your call and appeared to be asleep. On the floor were several cans of 'Special Brew', apparently empty. Alun eventually woke when you touched his arm. He smelled strongly of drink and appeared disorientated. He seemed not to recognise you. His speech was slurred and he had difficulty in rising to his feet. He eventually told you, in reply to your questioning, that Tracy was upstairs. She also appeared to be asleep. She had a black eye and a scratch on her right cheek. You could not rouse her.

Taking John with you, you went to the phone box at the end of the road and called an ambulance and the police. Upon returning to the house you found that Alun had gone back to sleep. The ambulance arrived before the police. Alan woke and started to shout at you and the ambulance crew. John was clearly very distressed and began to cry. This seemed to make Alun even more aggressive and you were relieved when the police arrived. Alun was blocking the doorway as they approached the house, preventing your exit and that of the ambulance crew who were trying to bring Tracy down the stairs. John was very distressed by this stage and Alun tried to take him out of your arms. A policeman tried to hold on to Alun's arm but Alun hit out at him. Alun was arrested.

The police exercised their powers under the Children Act 1989 (Section 46) and escorted you to Southtown General Hospital with John. You were joined at the hospital by a colleague who stayed with John while you went to secure an emergency protection order (EPO), which you successfully did by application to a single magistrate at around 4.00pm.

John was admitted to the paediatric ward at Southtown General that same afternoon, shortly after your return. Upon examination he was found to weigh just under 9kg and, in the opinion of the paediatrician, to be severely developmentally delayed. You were told that the marks that you saw were bruises at different stages of healing and that they were consistent with a sharp blow to the side of the head and to being gripped very tightly around the back of the neck and on the leg. The paediatrician also told you that there were other marks on John's back, consistent with being hit with a strap. He told you that, in his opinion, all of the injuries were consistent with non-accidental injury and that the police should be informed. In the view of the paediatrician, John will need nursing care for at least four to six weeks on an in-patient basis as he has so much weight to gain. John has quietened down and is asleep by the time that you leave the hospital at around 7.00pm.

It transpires that Tracy had taken an overdose of pain-killers and was admitted overnight to the same hospital as John. Alun was detained overnight in police cells but was bailed the next morning. He was re-arrested after his appearance in court and was charged with the assault on John. He appeared in court for the second time later in the day and was remanded on bail for a week, despite police objections.

On the next day (5th) you visited Tracy in hospital. She appeared horrified to hear of the bruises to John and denied all knowledge of them. Tracy says that she intends to return to Alun as soon as she can and will take John with her. She says that she does not want to see you again and that she does not need or want any help from you or your agency. Tracy seems to believe that Alun was attacked by the police and even suggests that the bruises to John may have been caused in the scuffle at the house. The ward sister told you that Tracy is very depressed and that she ought to stay in hospital for a few days. However, Tracy discharged herself later that day. John remained in hospital under the terms of the EPO. Tracy visited her mother to tell her, according to a later conversation you had with Mrs. Taylor (senior), that she no longer wanted anything to do with her mother, whom she blamed for 'causing all this trouble'. Tracy returned home to Alun.

The strength of the relationship between John and his mother is acknowledged and the importance of continued contact with her is recognised in allowing her unrestricted access to him in hospital. You want to work in partnership with Tracy, and, possibly, even with Alun, to ensure that John's welfare is safeguarded and promoted but decide that the partnership needs to be an unequal one at this stage and that you need to be able to determine how far Tracy and Alun can be involved in parenting John at this point in their lives. Accordingly, with the agreement of an Initial Child Abuse Case Conference, it is decided to make application for a Care Order in respect of John. His name is also entered on the Child Protection Register.

 **THE CARE ORDER**

The remainder of this Unit will focus on the process of applying for a care order in respect of John. We have chosen to do this not necessarily because we consider this the typical or inevitable outcome of such cases nor because we believe that a care order has a particular significance above that of other orders but principally so that we can explore in greater depth what is involved in securing one particular order rather than take a wider, but necessarily more superficial, view of the range of possible outcomes in this case.

The decision to make such an application must never be taken lightly or without proper consideration by a multi-disciplinary case conference. *The Children Act 1989 Guidance and Regulations Volume 1 Court Orders* (DOH 1991e, para.3.10) makes it clear that:

> no decision to initiate proceedings should be taken without clear evidence that provision of services for the child and his family...has failed or would be likely to fail to meet the child's needs adequately...and that there is no suitable person prepared to take over the care of the child under a residence order.

The question for the local authority must be: 'What will the use of compulsory powers add in safeguarding the child and is the gain sufficient to justify the use of compulsion and the trauma that may result' (DOH 1991e, para3.11).

In the artificial circumstances of the Taylor case we are not able to judge entirely satisfactorily that the decision to apply for a care order was the only or best alternative. Guidance (DOH 1991e, para. 1.12) states that 'where the prognosis for change is reasonable and the parents show a willingness to co-operate with voluntary arrangements, an application for a care order...is unlikely to succeed'.

For the purposes of the remainder of this Unit, we will ask you to assume that the prognosis for change is not good, although you will have an opportunity to further reflect on this in Exercise 10.1.

But, what precisely is a care order? The following Study Text offers an abbreviated account.

Study Text 10.1: The Care Order

EFFECT AND DURATION

When a care order is made with respect to a child it becomes the duty of the local authority named in the order to receive that child into its care (s.33(1)) and to accommodate him and maintain him during the currency of the order and to safeguard and promote his welfare (s.22(3)). The local authority will assume parental responsibility for the child and acquire the power to determine how far others shall be allowed to exercise their parental responsibility in respect of the child (s.33(3)). Proceedings for a care order cannot be brought before the birth of a child or after the age of 17 (16 if married) and no care order can last beyond the child's 18th birthday (s.31(3)).

THE COURT'S DECISION

The decision of the court to make a care order or not is taken in two stages: first, the court must decide whether the statutory 'threshold' criteria have been satisfied and, second, that the principles contained in Part I of the

Act have been applied. The 'threshold' criteria relate to whether the child has suffered, or is likely to suffer, 'significant harm' (see below). The relevant Part I principles are that the child's welfare must be the court's paramount consideration (s.1(1)), understood in the light of the 'welfare check-list' (s.1(3)) (see Study Text 1.3). This 'check-list' requires the court to consider, for example, the wishes and feelings of the child, the child's physical, emotional and educational needs and to have regard to the range of powers at its disposal. The court must also determine that making an order will be 'better for the child than making no order at all' (s.1(5)). The court will also have regard to arrangements for the child to have contact with parents or others (s.34(11)).

THE THRESHOLD CRITERIA

Section 31(2) of the Act establishes that:

A court may only make a care order or supervision order if it is satisfied-

(a) that the child concerned is suffering, or is likely to suffer, significant harm: and

(b) that the harm, or likelihood of harm is attributable to -

(i) the care given to the child, or likely to be given to him if the order were not made, not being what it would be reasonable to expect a parent to give to him; or

(ii) the child's being beyond parental control

By 'is suffering' is meant at the point of the hearing, or the point at which the local authority initiated the procedure to protect the child, provided that whatever arrangements were put in place then have remained in place. In the case of John Taylor, assuming that the EPO is still in force and/ or an interim care order was made, the time at issue would include the day of your visit to his home. By 'likely to suffer', the House of Lords has ruled (*Re H and Others (Child Sexual Abuse: Standard of Proof) [1996] 1 All ER, 1, [1996] 1 FLR 80.*) that in s.31 '…likely is being used in the sense of a real possibility, a possibility that cannot sensibly be ignored having regard to the nature and gravity of the feared harm…'. 'Harm' is defined (s.31(9)) as meaning 'ill-treatment or the impairment of health or development', where development means 'physical, intellectual, emotional, social or behavioural development', health means 'physical or mental health' and ill-treatment includes 'sexual abuse and forms of abuse which are not physical'. You should note that ill-treatment without consequent impairment may still constitute harm.

The Act does not offer a gloss on 'significant'. *The Children Act 1989 Guidance and Regulations Volume 1 Court Orders* (DOH 1991e) relies on a dictionary definition of 'significant' as meaning 'considerable, noteworthy or important' (para.3.19). Note that it is the harm which has to be significant, not whatever act caused it. Hence, a sustained series of privations, not individually harmful, as in the case of neglect, could amount to significant harm as far as the child's development was concerned. Not all harm will be significant nor will significant harm in one context necessarily be significant in another. Ultimately, it is a matter for the court to determine whether the harm is significant for the particular child in question. In those circumstances where the harm is said to be to the child's health or development, the court must compare it with what could be reasonably expected of a similar child (s.31(10)). A 'similar child' is one with the same attributes, needs and potential of the child in question, taking into account, for example, any particular learning or physical disability.

The harm caused to the child must be attributable to the care given to the child or to its being beyond parental control. The test of what would 'be reasonable to expect a parent to give him' is an objective one and does not depend on the motives or capacity of the carer. A parent may be trying very hard but still not be able to provide an adequate standard of care (you should note that s.105 of the Act establishes the foregoing as the definition of significant harm for the remaining purposes of the Act, including when used to form the grounds of an application for an Emergency Protection Order or for the purposes of a s.47 investigation – see Unit 9).

PROCESS

Most public law applications under the Act will be commenced in the Family Proceedings Court (C(AP)(A)O 1994 Art. 3). Figure 10. 1 sets out the court structure for proceedings under the Children Act 1989. The application must be made on the prescribed form. The form is divided into nine sections and seeks information under the following headings:

- the child – e.g. name, address, representation
- the applicant – as above

HOUSE OF LORDS

The House of Lords hears appeals from the Court of Appeal and from the High Court

---

COURT OF APPEAL (CIVIL DIVISION)

The Court of Appeal hears appeals from the High Court and County Court

---

HIGH COURT (FAMILY DIVISION)

The High Court deals with private and public law cases where there are complex points of law involved; applications by children in private law matters; wardship and appeals from the Family Proceedings Court.

COUNTY COURT

Almost all private law applications begin here.

There are three broad categories of County Court as far as proceedings under the Children Act are concerned:

Divorce Centres, which may determine applications under Parts I and II of the Act, apart from contested s8 orders

Family Hearing Centres, which deal with applications under Parts I and II of the Act, including contested s8 orders

Care Centres, which may determine both private and public law matters, including applications under Parts III, IV and V of the Act transferred from the Family Proceedings Court

---

FAMILY PROCEEDINGS COURT

Almost all public law cases and some private law matters begin here.

Figure 10.1: Court structure

- the child's family – e.g. marital status of parents, brothers and sisters
- whether a court-directed investigation has been ordered in the case
- distribution of parental responsibility
- any other applications that affect the child – e.g. if an EPO is in force, details of any pre-existing orders
- the basis of the application itself – e.g. nature of grounds on which application is based and any directions required if an interim order is to be made
- plans for the child if the order is made.

The final section of the form requires the applicant to declare that the information given is 'correct and complete' to the best of their knowledge.

Once the form has been received by the court, the court must fix a date either for the hearing of the case or, much more likely, for a directions hearing to be held. The court will then return copies of the forms to the applicant so that one can be served on all of those persons who have standing in the case. A full copy of the application (and the date fixed for the directions or full hearing) must be served on everyone with parental responsibility for the child and the child itself, that is to say to the 'automatic respondents' in the case. Other people can apply to the court and become full respondents and have a voice in proceedings. Certain people are entitled to receive notice of the application and be informed of the date, time and place of the hearing but not to receive details of the application. These include parents without parental responsibility and any person with whom the child was living before the application was begun.

The directions hearing is a formal procedure designed to minimise delay in such proceedings. It is attended by both the applicant, the respondents and/or their representatives, although usually not by the child concerned. Rules (*Family Proceedings Courts (Children Act 1989) Rules 1991, r 14(2)*) establish what kind of directions can be given. They include:

- the timetable for proceedings
- whether the child is to attend the hearing
- the appointment of a guardian *ad litem*
- arrangements for the submission of evidence.

We will return to the submission of evidence in Study Text 10.2.

THE GUARDIAN AD LITEM

Guidance (DOH 1991h, para.2.1) defines the function of the Guardian *ad Litem* and Reporting Officer (GALRO) as: 'to safeguard and promote the interests of the child by providing independent social work investigation and advice to the courts in care, child protection, adoption and related court proceedings'.

The Guardian *ad Litem*, drawn from an independent panel of GALs administered, but not managed, by the local authority will usually, but not necessarily, be a qualified and experienced social worker. They will have been appointed 'as soon as practicable' (*The Family Proceedings Courts (Children Act 1989) Rules 1991 r. 10 (1)*) in the legal process and will be asked their advice not only on matters relating to the interests of the child but also on such matters as the appropriate forum for the proceedings, the timetable for proceedings and the range of options that might be used to best resolve the matter before the court (Rules 11 (4)(c–f)). In reaching their opinion on how the child's interests might best be served, the GAL will consult with those whom they or the court see fit (Rules 11(9)(a)), have access to local authority records concerning the child (Children Act s.42) and obtain such professional advice and assistance as they determine appropriate (Rules 11(9)(c)). They will also consult with the child on a wide range of matters but GALs are not bound by the child's views in forming their opinion on what is in the child's interests. The GAL will usually appoint a solicitor to represent the child (Rules 11(2)) unless the solicitor is of the opinion, or the court directs, that the child instruct the solicitor on its own behalf. The range of proceedings in which a Guardian may be appointed is extensive (s.41 (6)) and, to all intents and purposes, will include most of the cases in which you, as a social worker, are likely to be involved. Courts are not obliged to appoint a GAL in every case where an appointment is permissible but must do so 'unless satisfied that it is not necessary to do so in order to safeguard [the child's] interests' (s.41 (1)).

POWERS OF THE COURT

Upon hearing an application for a care order, the court has access to the full range of orders available under the Act. Accordingly, the court may make any of the following orders *in addition* to a care order:

- parental responsibility order (if applied for)
- appointment (termination) of guardianship order
- care contact order (s.34).

The court may also, on refusing a care order, make a supervision order or any of the orders listed above or any s.8 order (see Appendix 1), with or without an application having been made.

OTHER CONSIDERATIONS

As well as having regard to the arrangements for contact with a child subject to a care order, case law (e.g. *Re J (Minors) (Care: Care Plan)[1994] 1 FLR 253*) has established that the local authority's plans for the child are also open to detailed scrutiny by the courts.

THE DECISION OF THE COURT

The court will reach its conclusions on matters of fact 'on the balance of probabilities', which means, in Lord Denning's famous dictum (*Miller v Ministry of Pensions [1947] 2 All ER 372*), that the court must be satisfied that it is 'more likely than not' that the particular events took place.

You may find the arrangement of material in this Study Text a useful template for your study of other orders under the Children Act 1989.

Exercise 10.1: Establishing the Grounds

This exercise is designed to give you an opportunity of familiarising yourself with the grounds on which a care order is made.

TASKS:

1. Examine recent entries in the Taylor Case File and determine whether a reasonable case can be made for the making of a care order in respect of John. You should structure your response as follows:

   - Is he suffering harm?
   - Is he likely to suffer harm?
   - What is the precise nature of the harm he is, or is likely to, suffer?

- Is it ill-treatment?
  - physical
  - sexual
  - mental
- Is it impairment of health?
  - physical
  - mental
- Is it impairment of development?
  - physical
  - emotional
  - behavioural
  - intellectual
  - social
- Is that harm significant?
- Is it attributable to the standard of care given to him?
- Is it attributable to the standard of care likely to be given to him?
- Is it attributable to his being beyond parental control?

2. Consider whether the use of compulsory powers is justified in this case. In particular, you might consider:

   - How can John's immediate and medium-term needs best be met, such that his welfare is properly safeguarded and protected?
   - What potential for change exists in John's carers' circumstances or capacity to provide for his needs?
   - What services would need to be provided in order to enable John to continue in the care of his parents?
   - What is the likely level of co-operation from Tracy, Alun and Mrs Taylor?

Points to Consider

1. How does the Children Act concept of 'significant harm' correspond with your definition of abuse? Is it a broader or a narrower definition?

2. Look back at the answers you gave in Exercise 6.2. Would an understanding of 'significant harm' have helped you to make your decisions more easily? Would it have made you make different decisions?

3. Would your understanding of 'significant harm' have helped you to determine more easily whether John was subject to abuse prior to this recent series of incidents?

4. Given your understanding of secondary risk factors (Study Text 9.2), what factors do you think influence decisions to make use of compulsory powers where you work?

5. Do you think that the threshold for making applications to the court is clearly and appropriately fixed where you work?

6. What does the fact that you have access to compulsory powers in this way tell you about the nature of your role at the boundaries of family, state and the law?

Once the decision is made to make an application for a care order, the procedural, management and administrative arrangements required to ensure that the necessary steps are taken, in the right order, will vary from area to area. In some local authorities the matter will be steered by the authority's legal advisors from a very early point in the process. Some local authorities, for example, arrange for legal advice to be available routinely at case conferences where decisions to make applications to the court are likely to arise. In other areas, social workers will be responsible for obtaining, completing and, in some cases, serving the relevant forms.

Whatever the arrangements, the social worker will have an important part to play in establishing the basis of the application through the evidence that they will offer the court. The following Study Text and

Exercise will familiarise you with what is required in the preparation of your evidence.

Study Text 10.2: Evidence

THE WITNESS STATEMENT

You may have noted that one of the considerations to be made at the directions hearing concerned the submission of evidence (*Family Proceedings Courts (Children Act 1989) Rules 1991 r. 14(2)(f)*). Rule 17 explains that parties to the proceedings (i.e. applicants and respondents) must file with the court, and serve on the remaining parties, 'written statements of the substance of the oral evidence which the party intends to adduce at a hearing…[and]…copies of any documents, including…experts' reports, upon which the party intends to rely…'. That is to say that you will have to prepare, in advance of the hearing and to the timetable established at the directions hearing, a comprehensive account of the evidence you intend to give at the hearing and co-ordinate the submission of any other reports that it is intended to use in pursuit of the application. Paragraph 3 of Rule 17 establishes that you will need the permission of the court to adduce additional evidence or seek to rely on a document that you have not filed with the court and served on the remaining parties. You may not be able to rely on your case notes, for example, unless you have previously filed them with the court or are prepared to have them scrutinised by the other parties' representatives, nor will you be allowed to call a mystery expert at the last dramatic moment. The principle of 'advance disclosure' is an important one in family proceedings.

It is clear just how important your witness statement will be. It will form the basis of the 'evidence in chief' that you will present to the court and on which you will be cross-examined; it will be closely read by the magistrates before the case and by the lawyers representing the respondents, as well as by family members. This Study Text will provide some guidance on the preparation of your witness statement but it will be necessary to first make some general points about evidence in civil proceedings.

THE RULES OF EVIDENCE

In order to be taken into account by a court making a decision in any matter before it, evidence must be relevant and admissible. In order to be relevant, the evidence must logically bear on proving or disproving the point at issue. Unless a particular exclusion applies, all relevant evidence is admissible. The general exclusions are hearsay evidence, evidence concerned with opinion and evidence concerned with character. However, in the case of proceedings under the Act, certain qualifications apply to these general exclusions (the rules of evidence relating to character apply largely to criminal proceedings and are not considered here.)

HEARSAY EVIDENCE

The general rule is that witnesses should give evidence of that which they have actually observed. Hearsay evidence is 'evidence of a statement made to a witness by a person who is not himself a witness' and is generally inadmissible. However, in order, particularly, to bring the evidence of children before the court in such a way that the child need not be present, *The Children (Admissibility of Hearsay Evidence) Order 1993* does allow such evidence where it relates to the upbringing, maintenance or welfare of the child to be admitted. This provision does not apply only to statements made by the child concerned. However, the court, which will always have a preference for the best and most direct evidence, will have to assess what weight to attach to hearsay evidence.

OPINION EVIDENCE

The general rule that witnesses should confine themselves to matters of fact and not offer an opinion does not apply when the opinion offered is that of an expert (in the view of the court) and that the opinion will be of use to the court in determining the matter in question. Expert witnesses, including social workers, will usually give evidence on matters of fact observed by them or interpretation of those or other facts adduced in evidence and offer an opinion on the significance of the facts or interpretation. All expert witnesses, again including social workers, must only offer opinions that they genuinely hold and not just those that favour one or other party to the proceedings. If you need to quote research evidence to support your opinion, do so sparingly and make sure that you are aware of what criticisms have been made of the original research.

PREPARING YOUR STATEMENT

Perhaps the most important point of all to bear in mind when preparing your witness statement is that you cannot make it better than the assessment that informs it or the work that has already gone into the case. You should not now be at the point of reading the case file for the first time or of imposing a structure on your knowledge of the family! You will need to re-read the file and refresh your memory as you compile your statement, of course. As part of this process you may identify material that you wish to rely on in your evidence, such as a piece of correspondence or a working agreement which could then be appended to your statement. But, the real preparation for drawing up your statement began when you were first allocated this case and committed yourself to working to the highest professional standards that both families and the court have a right to expect of you.

If it is the case that you cannot make a witness statement better than the thinking and the work that has preceded it, the converse certainly does not hold. It is perfectly possible to prepare a witness statement that makes well thought out and skilfully delivered work seem confused and poorly planned. Witness statements need time to prepare and you will need to rid yourself of as many distractions as you can in order to concentrate on researching, thinking and writing the statement. You should try to 'block out' at least two or three days for the purpose.

GENERAL ADVICE

- *Stick to the point.* It is a more demanding task to select relevant material that you wish to present to the court than to include everything you ever knew about the family and the practice of social work. In the Taylor case, it is not relevant to anything that Ron is a mechanic and so was his brother-in-law! Extraneous material obscures more than it reveals.

- *Differentiate between fact and opinion.* Consider the following sentence: 'When I arrived at the house, John was in danger from the traffic on the main road as he was playing, unattended, in an un-gated garden'. It is a matter of fact that John was playing in the garden with easy access to the main road but it is a matter of opinion as to whether that was potentially dangerous.

- *Make sure that any opinion you offer is within your competence* (i.e. within your observations and professional expertise). Consider this sentence: 'When I entered the living room, Mr. Evans, who was drunk, lay asleep on the sofa'. You are not competent to judge Alun Evans' state of intoxication (certainly not when he is asleep!). You are not a doctor nor do you have any knowledge or training that would enable you to determine his state of mental or physical alertness.

- *Wherever possible, let the facts speak for themselves.* Compare the following statement with the one above and decide which is the most helpful to the court in understanding what you saw and what subsequently happened: 'I observed Mr Evans lying on the sofa. There were a number of empty beer cans on the floor around him. Upon my waking him, he appeared disorientated and his speech was slurred'.

- *Clearly distinguish between hearsay and direct evidence.* Compare the following statements: (1) 'Ms Taylor later denied that Mr Evans had hit John, although previously she had said that Mr Evans was responsible for the bruises to John'. (2) 'I was informed by Mrs. Taylor (Senior) that her daughter had told her that Mr Evans had hit Ms Taylor and John. Mrs. Taylor reported this conversation to me on the 4th August during the course of a telephone call requesting that I visit her grandson. Mrs Taylor seemed very agitated during the course of the telephone conversation and expressed her concern for the well-being of both Ms Taylor and John. During the course of an interview with Ms Taylor, conducted by me on the 6th August whilst Ms Taylor was still a patient in Southtown General Hospital, Ms Taylor said that she did not know anything about the bruises to John and suggested to me that they may have been caused during the incident which led to the arrest of Mr Evans'. It is important that the court is fully aware of the circumstances in which hearsay evidence was gathered in order to determine what weight to attach to it.

- *Present a balanced account.* You have a duty to tell the whole truth to the court and not simply to select those 'facts' which fit your case. Consider these versions of the same event: (1) 'I first became involved with the Taylor Family when arrangements for the care of her two older children had reached the point of breakdown'. (2) 'Ms Taylor referred herself to the social services department, seeking help to manage difficulties that had arisen concerning the upbringing of her two older children'.

- *Avoid jargon.* What does the following actually mean? 'The dysfunctional relationship between the two older siblings and Ms Taylor's former spouse had expressed itself in acting-out behaviour on Michael's part'.

- *Use language that is respectful, authoritative and which you understand and with which you feel comfortable.* You will need to ensure that the importance of your statement is reflected in the tone that you adopt, but resist the temptation to write in your 'telephone voice'. Use family names and polite forms of address and make sure that your grammar and spelling are of the highest order. What might the following tell the court about the author of the statements? (1) 'I implied from what Tracy said to her mum that John had got his bruises from Alun who hit him the previous day when she spoke to me on the 'phone'. (2) 'I had facilitated access for Tracy and John to the local family treatment resource. This she had not availed herself of'. Neither of these statements would tell the court very much about the facts of the case.

STRUCTURE OF THE STATEMENT

Your agency may well have a favoured format for witness statements of this sort and may require you to use existing pro-formas. If not, the following (adapted from Plotnikoff and Woolfson 1996) may be of use:

1. Cover sheet and declaration: This should provide all the identifying detail that will ensure that the statement arrives at the right place at the right time as well as information on how to contact you. You will also have to make a declaration, as required by the Rules, declaring the truth of the statement and your knowledge that it may be placed before the court.

2. The author's credentials: A very brief statement of your qualifications and experience.

3. The statement's provenance: This should include a brief history of your involvement with this family and the sources that you have consulted in compiling your statement.

4. A 'cast list': Compile an index of all of those whose name appears in the statement and a brief identifying description. You might also include at this stage a detailed account of family structure and relationships, possibly using a genogram.

5. A chronology: This should be a chronology of key events that have a material bearing on the case. It will probably extend to include details of the births of all three children but need not, at this stage, go back as far as Tracy's own childhood. If it is decided to include a more detailed account of Tracy's past, this is best done within the body of the statement. Include critical incidents and dates of case conferences, planning meetings, etc.

6. The substantive case: This should include a detailed history of your involvement with the family as well as any more recent precipitating events. It is helpful if this section is broken down into sub-sections dealing, in turn, with the family, the child and the issues giving rise to concern. Information about the parents should include an account of their capacity to look after the child, their response to services and support already offered and their wishes and feelings for the future. Information about the child should include a consideration of all of those matters referred to in the 'welfare check-list' and those matters referred to in s22(5)(c), CA 1989 requiring a full consideration of the child's racial, cultural, religious and linguistic background.

7. Your assessment of risk: This should include a consideration of possible alternatives to the action that you are now asking the court to allow as well as a thorough account of those primary risk factors that have been demonstrated in the case.

8. The care plan: This should include arrangements for contact and must be described in a way that follows directly from your previous assessment of the child's needs, the capacity of its parents to meet them and your consideration of alternative courses of action. You must demonstrate to the court's satisfaction that what you intend will accord with the court's duty to have the child's welfare as its

paramount concern and that this can best be achieved by the making of the order that you seek.

9. Conclusion: This should provide a concise statement of the reasons for the application before the court and demonstrate that your proposed course of action is the most appropriate in this case.

Exercise 10.2: Writing a Witness Statement

Using the material included in Units 7–10, and the structure recommended in the previous Study Text, write a full witness statement to support an application for a care order in respect of John Taylor.

Points to Consider

1. Is your conclusion a convincing argument that the making of a care order is necessary to adequately safeguard and promote John's welfare?

2. Do your plans for John reflect the need to exercise compulsory powers?

3. Do you feel confident in the opinions that you offer?

4. Are these opinions based on, and justified by, the facts of the case?

5. Can you ground your opinions in an established body of social work knowledge?

6. Does your statement represent your honest belief that the course of action proposed will allow the court to fairly discharge its burden to have John's welfare as its paramount consideration?

GIVING EVIDENCE

The process of compiling a witness statement is a complex and daunting one. Once you have finished it, however, provided that it is based on competent practice and a well considered analysis, your confidence in the course of action you are about to undertake should begin to rise. If you are not confident that what you are asking the court to sanction is, in all the circumstances, the best course of action open to you in order to safeguard and promote the welfare of the child concerned, then you must seek professional advice immediately. In any well considered case there will be some residual uncertainty, of course, but if you are not convinced that what you propose will enable the court to make the order with the child's welfare as its paramount consideration then you should not be asking the court for such a decision.

Your confidence in your plans for the child and its family may not, however, equate to confidence in your own ability as a witness during the course of the hearing. The following Study Text offers some guidance on giving oral evidence. It begins with a brief account of the procedures likely to be encountered in the court room and a description of who else may be present.

Study Text 10.3: In the Box

COURTROOM LAYOUT AND KEY PERSONNEL

Almost invariably, proceedings such as the one we are simulating will commence in the Family Proceedings Court. The physical layout of such courts varies considerably, not least with the age of the court building, but, generally speaking, the 'bench' of magistrates (usually three) will sit together facing the 'well' of the court. It is the magistrates alone who determine matters of fact in proceedings and who decide what order(s), if any, to make. The court clerk, who will be legally qualified, will usually sit in front of the bench but sufficiently close to be able to speak to the bench easily. The court clerk is there to advise the bench on points of law and procedure and quite often will act as 'ringmaster' in the court. S/he is assisted by one or more ushers who will call witnesses, direct them to the witness box and administer the oath or affirmation. Usually facing the bench will sit the lawyers representing the various parties to the proceedings. Sometimes, the party from whom they are 'receiving instructions' will sit behind them but it is not uncommon for parties to be excluded at various points in the proceedings. The general public will not be allowed into the courtroom. Usually present throughout will be the guardian *ad litem*.

PROCEDURE IN THE COURTROOM

The evidence is usually 'adduced' in the following order, although the court can direct otherwise:

- the applicant
- any party with parental responsibility
- other respondents (e.g. unmarried father)
- the guardian *ad litem*
- the child (if not a party and there is no guardian *ad litem*).

Closing speeches are usually in the following order:

- other respondents
- any party with parental responsibility
- the applicant
- the guardian *ad litem*
- the child (if not a party and there is no guardian *ad litem*).

Once called to give evidence, you will be asked to take an oath or make an affirmation that the evidence you are about to give will be truthful. Your legal representative will then question you on the basis of the written statement you have filed with the court and which will form the basis of your 'evidence in chief'. Even though almost everyone in the room will have read your statement, the evidence it contains will be brought out in the course of this 'examination'. You will then be 'cross-examined' on the evidence you have given by the legal representatives of the other parties to the proceedings. The express purpose of this process is to test your evidence and, where it is weak or open to other interpretations, to make that clear to the court. Your legal representative may then re-examine you. This re-examination is not to adduce fresh evidence but to clarify any possible confusion or misunderstandings that may have arisen as a result of your cross-examination.

GIVING EVIDENCE

One important way in which courts evaluate the credibility and reliability of a piece of evidence is by the reliability and credibility of the witness. In other words, how you are perceived will strongly influence how much weight can be attached to what you have to say. Managing your 'perform-ance' in the witness box is a skill that develops with experience. For present purposes, bearing in mind all of the points made in relation to the presentation of written submissions, we offer the following 'do's' and 'don'ts':

- *Do* think hard about what impression your clothing and demeanour will make on the court. If you arrive breathless, bedraggled and spilling papers on the floor (it has been known!), you will look as disorganised and ill-prepared as you probably are. Courtrooms are probably less formal than they used to be but everyone else will be dressed soberly, recognising the seriousness of the business in hand. If you turn up in clothes more suited for the beach you will attract the same kind of opinion as if you turned up for the beach in a dark suit. Remember, the court will only have what they hear and see before them to help them make up their minds about you and what you have to say.

- *Do* address your evidence to the bench. All of your answers are for the benefit of the whole court, not just the questioner. There are a number of things you can do to remind yourself to address the bench. Position your feet facing towards the bench when you enter the witness box. Then, as you begin to respond to questions, even if you have turned to hear what the questioner is asking, your body will naturally return to face in the direction of your feet. Alternatively, you can begin your answers with the words 'Your Worships, I…'. This, again, will have the effect of making you turn towards the bench.

- *Don't* engage the lawyer asking you questions in conversation. Although it is 'natural' to wish to respond directly to the person asking you questions, an experienced advocate will be looking for visual clues from you in order to know when to interrupt. If you have not finished your answer, it is much easier to continue if it is your 'conversation' with the bench that the advocate has interrupted. It is the lawyer who will be disadvantaged if s/he appears to be rude. Engaging the bench, rather than your inquisitor, helps to avoid confrontation too.

- *Do* make sure that you can be heard. You can use the taking of the oath to 'warm up' your voice. Remember also that a great deal of additional information can be imparted through the tone of voice used. An expressive voice will secure greater attention than a flat monotone.

- *Don't* allow yourself to be flustered. Sort your notes out well in advance. Label them if you need to and make liberal use of a text marker. If you need to, ask permission to consult your notes, then do so carefully. If the questioner is pushing you along at too fast a pace or not allowing you to say what you want, try to impose a structure on your answers. One tried and tested technique is to reply: 'Your Worships, there are four points I would like to make in reply to that question…'. If you run out of 'points', either say so or say that you have substantially dealt with them in what you have already said.

- *Do* tell the truth! If you don't know the answer to a question, or cannot remember, say so. If you find yourself saying something that is misleading, untrue or incomplete, or if your questioner creates the impression that you believe something that you do not, then you must say so.

- *Don't* be taken by surprise. You should be able to predict, with a reasonable degree of accuracy, what the difficult questions are likely to be. Why did you not make more frequent visits to the Taylor Family after the two older children had left? Why did you not do more to ensure Tracy attended the Health Centre?

What happened to the place at the Family Centre that you had promised but not delivered?

- *Do* be ready to deal with alternative explanations of events. As an expert witness, you will be allowed to give your opinion on certain matters. This means that you should predict what other inferences could be drawn from the facts and be ready with an account of why your opinion contains the correct interpretation.

There are not many situations in life when the express purpose of the person asking you questions is to cast doubt on everything you say. Of course it is uncomfortable. Quite often it is meant to be. Remember, however, that you and your evidence are vital to the court's decision making. However uncomfortable you may feel, you have an important job to do and a perfect right to have your evidence, your professional expertise and personal integrity respected by the court. In one sense, giving evidence is no more than a continuation of professional practice by other means:

> The witness who is regarded as serious, caring, undogmatic, well-informed, fair and reasonable, and who shows respect for the family concerned, will be effective in helping the court to establish what is in the child's best interests... It is not suggested that [these qualities] can be acquired for the limited purpose of giving evidence. (Biggs and Robson 1992, p.13)

 **CONCLUSION**

The decision to proceed to court in furtherance of your duty to safeguard and promote the welfare of children with whom you are working should never be taken lightly or alone. In reaching your decision you will need to seek and consider the advice of senior colleagues and of specialists in other fields than your own. This can be a testing process whereby your judgement and your expertise may be questioned. We assume that you would not wish it any other way.

Similarly, when invoking the powers of the court is the best and most appropriate route to securing the welfare of a child and we would not wish you to shy away from your responsibilities. Going to court is an integral part of social work with children and families. Good social workers are good social workers just as much in the witness box as they are in case conferences, team meetings or in direct work with families. It is only the other kind that need have any concerns.

NOTES AND SELF-ASSESSMENT

1. What might the court process do to your future relationship with the child or family concerned? What can you do to maintain an effective relationship?

2. Who is most/least powerful or influential in the court process, do you think? Who should be?

3. Do you think that a courtroom is the most appropriate place in which to resolve complex family problems?

4. What does 'justice' mean in the context of family proceedings?

5. What impression do you want to make in court?

6. How close is that impression to the reality?

RECOMMENDED READING

Biggs, V. and Robson, J. (1992) *Developing your Court Skills*. London: BAAF.

Plotnikoff, J. and Woolfson, R. (1996) *Reporting to Court under the Children Act*. London: HMSO.

Pizzey, S. and Davis, J. (1995) *A Guide for Guardians ad Litem in Public Law Proceedings under the Children Act 1989*. London: HMSO.

TRAINER'S NOTES

Exercise 10.1: Establishing the Grounds

This exercise can best be undertaken by a group, either as a debate or in the form of a simulated case conference, strategy meeting or professional supervision session. The Trainer will need to be able to offer expert advice and allocate roles accordingly. In a simulated case conference it is sometimes difficult for participants to role play family members or the child concerned. If this is the case, John's interests can be represented by a guardian *ad litem* (adjusting the fiction a little so that the meeting takes place after the directions hearing). Other members of the group should observe the interactions and imaginatively recreate what this might signify for Tracy and Alun, without becoming actively involved in the drama. This arrangement is closer to what might usually happen in reality.

Exercise 10.2: Writing a Witness Statement

This is a difficult exercise to manage with a large group. However, the most effective way of testing the witness statement, and the court skills described in Study Text 10.3, is to simulate the hearing itself. If at all possible, such an exercise should take place in a real courtroom. These can be hired (and can be quite expensive!) through your Court Clerk's Office or through the Administrator for the county court in your area. It is possible to re-arrange the furniture and simulate a courtroom elsewhere but something of the sense of atmosphere and occasion is lost in the process. The Trainer should try to secure the services of an experienced local solicitor specialising in family matters to appear on behalf of Tracy. The Trainer can act as the solicitor representing the local authority. It is not necessary to rehearse the whole hearing. The most important element is to provide participants with the opportunity to have their evidence adduced and to be cross-examined by someone with the necessary skills and with whom they have no previous acquaintance. The greater the verisimilitude (including insistence on the appropriate dress code), the more useful participants will find the exercise. Trainers may be surprised by the degree of anxiety demonstrated by participants.

APPENDIX I
Orders under the Children Act 1989

The following is a thumbnail description of all of the orders that may be made under the Children Act 1989, except those orders concerning financial provisions.

Order	Section	Description
Parental responsibility order	s.4	Gives an unmarried father parental responsibility for his child
Appointment of guardian	s.5	Appoints a person as a child's guardian
Termination of appointment of guardian	s.6	Terminates the appointment of a child's guardian
Residence order	s.8	Settles the arrangements as to with whom a child shall live
Section 8 contact order	s.8	Directs a child's carer to allow the child contact with another person
Prohibited steps order	s.8	Prevents a specific step that might be taken in relation to the exercise of parental responsibility
Specific issue order	s.8	Resolves a specific issue in relation to any aspect of the exercise of parental responsibility
Family assistance order	s.16	Requires a probation officer or officer of the local authority to advise, assist and befriend a named person

Order	Section	Description
Secure accommodation order	s.25	Authorises the admission of a child to accommodation for the purpose of restricting liberty
Care order	s.31	Places a child in the care of a named local authority (see Unit 10)
Supervision order	s.31	Places a child under the supervision of a local authority or probation officer
Care contact order	s.34	Regulates contact between a child in care and a named person
Education supervision order	s.36	Places a child under the supervision of a named local education authority
Interim care/supervision order	s.38	Temporary order made during the course of proceedings
Child assessment order	s.43	Directs and authorises an assessment of the child's health, development or the way in which the child is treated
Emergency protection order	s.44	Directs the protection of the child and authorises either the removal of the child to suitable accommodation or prevents the removal of the child from the place at which s/he is currently accommodated
Recovery order	s.50	Provides for the recovery of a child in care or who is subject to an EPO or police protection and who has been abducted or has run away

APPENDIX 2
Index to Exercises

APPENDIX 3

Index to Study Texts

References

Abbott, P. (1989) 'Family lifestyles and structures.' In W.S. Rogers, D. Hevey and E. Ash (eds) *Child Abuse and Neglect – Facing the Challenge.* Milton Keynes: OUP.

Adcock, M. and White, R. (eds) (1985) *Good-enough Parenting – a Framework for Assessment.* London: BAAF.

Ahmad, B. (1990) *Black Perspectives in Social Work.* Birmingham: Venture Press.

Anderson, S. (1984) 'Goal setting in social work practice.' In B.R. Compton and B. Galaway (1984) (eds) *Social Work Processes.* Chicago: Dorsey Press.

Archard, D. (1993) *Children – Rights and Childhood.* London: Routledge.

Aries, P. (1960) *L'Enfant et la vie familiale sous l'ancien regime.* Paris: Libraire Plon. Translated by Baldick, R. as *Centuries of Childhood* (1962). London: Jonathon Cape.

Arnstein, R.A. (1972) 'Power to the people: an assessment of the community action and model cities experience.' *Public Administration Review 32,* 377–389.

Atherton, C. and Dowling, P. (1989) 'Using written agreements: the family's point of view.' In J. Aldgate (ed) *Using Written Agreements with Children and Families.* London: FRG.

Biggs, V. and Robson, J. (1992) *Developing your Court Skills.* London: BAAF.

Bowlby, J. (1970) *Attachment.* New York: Basic Books.

Braye, S. and Preston-Shoot, N. (1992) *Practising Social Work Law.* London: Macmillan.

Brayne, H. and Martin, G. (1990) (3rd edition) *Law for Social Workers.* London: Blackstone Press.

British Social Attitudes Survey (1983) London: HMSO.

British Social Attitudes Survey (1984) London: HMSO.

British Social Attitudes Survey (1987) London: HMSO.

British Social Attitudes Survey (1991) London: HMSO.

Brook, E. and Davis, A. (1985) (eds) *Women, The Family and Social Work.* London: Tavistock.

Bryer, M. (1988) *Planning in Child Care.* London: BAAF.

Bullock, R., Little, M. and Milham, S. (1993) *Residential Care for Children – A Review of the Research.* London: HMSO.

Burden, D.S. and Gottlieb, N. (1987) (eds) *The Woman Client.* London: Tavistock.

273

Butler, I. (1996a) 'Children and the sociology of childhood.' In I. Butler and I. Shaw (eds) *A Case of Neglect? Children's Experiences and the Sociology of Childhood.* Aldershot: Avebury.

Butler, I. (1996b) 'Safe? Involving children in child protection.' In I. Butler and I. Shaw (eds) *A Case of Neglect? Children's Experiences and the Sociology of Childhood.* Aldershot: Avebury.

Butler, I. and Owens, D. (1993) 'Canaries among sparrows: ideas of the family and the practice of family care.' *Community Alternatives: International Journal of Family Care 5,* 1, 25–43.

Butler, I. and Williamson, H. (1994) *Children Speak: Children, Trauma and Social Work.* London: Longman.

Butler, I., Noaks, L., Douglas, G., Lowe, N. and Pithouse, A. (1993) 'The Children Act and the Issue of Delay.' *Family Law 23,* 412–414.

CCESTW (1995) *Assuring Quality in the Diploma in Social Work – 1 Rules and Requirements for the DipSW.* London: CCETSW.

Central Statistical Office (1994) *Social Trends 24.* London: HMSO.

Cheal, D. (1991) *Family and the State of Theory.* Hemel Hempstead: Harvester Wheatsheaf.

Cheetham, J. (1986) 'Introduction.' In S. Ahmed, J. Cheetham and J. Small (eds) *Social Work with Black Children and their Families.* London: Batsford.

Clement-Brown, S. (1947) 'Foreword.' In D.M. Dyson. *The Foster Home and the Boarded Out Child.* London: George, Allen and Unwin.

Cleveland Report (1988) *Report of the Inquiry into Child Abuse in Cleveland.* (Butler-Sloss LJ). London: HMSO.

Cloke, C. and Davies, M. (1995) *Participation and Empowerment in Child Protection.* London: Pitman.

Clyde Report (1992) *Report of the Inquiry into the Removal of Children from Orkney in February 1991.* Edinburgh: HMSO.

Coit, K. (1978) 'Local action not citizen participation.' In W. Tabb and L. Sawers (ed) *Marxism and the Metropolis.* New York: Oxford University Press.

Compton, B.R. and Galaway, B. (1984) (eds) *Social Work Processes.* Chicago: Dorsey Press.

Cooper, C. (1985) 'Good-enough, border line and bad-enough parenting.' In M. Adcock and R. White (eds) *Good Enough Parenting: A Framework for Assessment.* London: BAAF.

Corob, A. (1987) *Working with Depressed Women.* Aldershot: Gower.

Coulshed, V. (1988) *Social Work Practice – An Introduction.* Basingstoke: Macmillan.

Cournoyer, B. (1991) *The Social Work Skills Workbook.* Belmont CA: Wadsworth.

Cox, D. and Parish, A. (1989) *Working in Partnership.* Barkingside, Barnardos.

Creighton, S. (1986) *Child abuse in 1985, Initial Findings from NSPCC Register Research.* London: NSPCC.

Daines, R., Lyons, K. and Parsloe, P. (1990) *Aiming for Partnership.* Ilford: Barnardos.

Davis, A., Llewellyn, S. and Parry, G. (1985) 'Women and mental health .' In E. Brook and A. Davis, Women, *The Family and Social Work.* London: Tavistock.

Davies, M. (1994) (3rd Edition) *The Essential Social Worker – A Guide to Positive Practice.* Aldershot: Gower.

Dewer, J. (1992) *Law and the Family,* (2nd Edition). London: Butterworths.

DHSS (1985) *Social Work Decisions in Child Care – Recent Research Findings and their Implications.* London: HMSO.

Dingwall, R. (1989) 'Some problems about predicting child abuse and neglect.' In O. Stevenson (ed) *Child Abuse: Public Policy and Professional Practice.* Hemel Hempstead: Harvester Wheatsheaf.

Directors of Social Work in Scotland (1992) *Child Protection: Policy Practice and Procedure.* Edinburgh: HMSO.

DOH (1988) *Protecting Children – A Guide for Social Workers Undertaking a Comprehensive Assessment.* London: HMSO.

DOH (1989) *An Introduction to the Children Act 1989.* London HMSO.

DOH (1990a) *The Care of Children – Principles and Practice in Regulations and Guidance.* London: HMSO.

DOH (1990b) *Child Care Policy – Putting it in Writing. A Review of Local Authorities', Child Care Policy Statements.* London: HMSO.

DOH (1991a) *The Children Act 1989 Guidance and Regulations Volume 3 Family Placements.* London: HMSO.

DOH (1991b) *Children Act 1989 Guidance and Regulations Volume 2 Family Support, Day Care and Educational Provision for Young Children.* London: HMSO.

DOH (1991c) *Patterns and Outcomes in Child Placement – Messages from Current Research and their Implications.* London: HMSO.

DOH (1991d) *Children Act 1989 Guidance and Regulations Volume 4 Residential Care.* London: HMSO.

DOH (1991e) *The Children Act 1989 Guidance and Regulations Volume 1 Court Orders.* London: HMSO.

DOH (1991f) *Residential Care for Children – Report of a Department of Health Seminar (30/09/91 – 01/11/91).* London: DOH.

DOH (1991g) *Working Together Under the Children Act 1989.* London: HMSO.

DOH (1991h) *The Children Act 1989 Guidance and Regulations Volume 7 Guardians ad Litem and other Court Related Issues.* London: HMSO.

DOH (1994) *Planning Long Term Placements Study.* London: HMSO.

DOH (1995a) *Child Protection – Messages from Research.* London: HMSO.

DOH (1995b) *Children Looked After by Local Authorities 14 October 1991 to 31 March 1993 England.* London: DOH/Government Statistical Service.

DOH (1996) *Children Looked After by Local Authorities Year Ending 31 March 1994 England.* London: DOH/Government Statistical Service.

Dominelli, L. (1988) *Anti-Racist Social Work.* London: Macmillan/BASW.

Dominelli, L. and Mcleod, E. (1989) *Feminist Social Work.* London: Macmillan.

Eekelaar, J. (1991) *Regulating Divorce.* London: OUP.

Elliot, F.R. (1986) *The Family – Change or Continuity?* London: Allen and Unwin.

European Network on Childcare (1996) *A Review of Childcare Services for Young Children in the EU 1990–1995.* Brussels: Equal Opportunities Unit.

Fahlberg, V. (1985) 'Checklists on attachment.' In M. Adcock and R. White (eds) *Good Enough Parenting: A Framework for Assessment.* London: BAAF.

Fahlberg, V. (1988) *Fitting the Pieces Together.* London: BAAF.

Firestone, S. (1979) 'Childhood is hell.' In M. Hoyles (ed) *Changing Childhood.* London: Writers and Readers Publishing Co-operative.

Fischoff, B., Lichtenstein, S., and Slovic, P. (1981) *Acceptable Risk.* Cambridge: Cambridge University Press.

Frankenburg, S. (1946) *Common Sense in the Nursery.* London: Penguin.

Franklin, B. (ed) (1995) *The Handbook of Children's Rights – Comparative Policy and Practice.* London: Routledge.

FRG (1989) *Using Written Agreements with Children and Families.* London: FRG.

Fry, S. (1993) 'The family curse.' In *Paperweight.* London: Manderin.

Gambe, D., Gomes, J., Kapur, V., Rangel, M. and Stubbs, P. (1992) *Improving Practice with Children and Families.* Leeds: CCETSW.

Gibbons, J., Thorpe, S. and Wilkinson, P. (1990) *Family Support and Prevention: Studies in Local Areas.* London: NISW.

Goffman, E. (1961) *Asylums.* New York: Doubleday.

Gough, D. (1993) *Child Abuse Interventions – A Review of the Research Literature.* Glasgow: Public Health Research Unit, University of Glasgow.

Greenland, C. (1987) *Preventing CAN Deaths: An International Study of Deaths Due to Child Abuse and Neglect.* London: Tavistock.

Hale, J. (1983) 'Feminism and social work practice.' In B. Jordan and N. Parton (eds) *The Political Dimensions of Social Work.* Oxford: Blackwell.

Hanmer, J. and Statham (1988) *Women and Social Work – Towards a Woman Centered Practice.* London: Macmillan.

Harris, C.C. (1984) *The Family and Industrial Society.* London: Allen and Unwin.

Hendrick, H. (1994) *Child Welfare England 1872–1989.* London: Routledge.

Hepworth, D.H. and Larsen, J.A. (1982) *Direct Social Work Practice: Theory and Skills.* Chicago: Dorsey Press.

Hoghughi, M. (1988) *Treating Problem Children – Issues, Methods and Practice*. London: Sage.

Holt, J. (1975) *Escape from Childhood – the Needs and Rights of Children*. London: Penguin.

Howe, D. (1987) *An Introduction to Social Work Theory*. Aldershot: Wildwood House.

Hoyles, M. (1979) (ed) *Changing Childhood*. London: Writers and Readers Publishing Co-operative.

Jackson, S. and Kilroe, S. (1996) *Looking After Children: Good Parenting, Good Outcomes – Reader*. London: HMSO.

James, A. and Prout, A. (1991) 'A new paradigm for the sociology of childhood? Provenance, promise and problems.' In A. James and A. Prout (eds) *Constructing and Reconstructing Childhood: Contemporary Issues in the Sociological Study of Childhood*. London: The Falmer Press.

Johnson, T. (1972) *Professions and Power*. London: Macmillan.

Joshi, H. (1992) 'The cost of caring.' In C. Glendinning and J. Millar (eds) *Women and Poverty in Britain in the 1990s*. Hemel Hempstead: Harvester Wheatsheaf.

Kates, V. (1985) 'Success, strain and surprise.' *Issues in Science and Technology* 2, 46–58.

Kellmer Pringle, M.L. (1974) *The Needs of Children*. London: Hutchinson.

Kennell, J., Voos, D. and Klaus, M. (1976) 'Parent–infant bonding.' In R. Helfer and C.H. Kempe (eds) *Child Abuse and Neglect*. Cambridge, Mass: Ballinger.

Langan, M. and Day, L. (1992) (eds) *Women, Oppression and Social Work – Issues in Anti-Discriminatory Practice*. London: Routledge.

Leech, P. (1994) *Children First: What our Society Must Do – and is Not Doing: For our Children Today*. London: Michael Joseph.

Lorde, A. (1984) *Sister Outsider*. New York: Crossing Press.

Macdonald, S. (1991) *All Equal Under the Act?* London: REU/NISW.

McCarthy, M. (1989) 'Personal social services.' In M. McCarthy (ed) *The New Politics of Welfare: An Agenda for the 1990s?* London: Macmillan.

Menzies, I.E.P. (1970) *The Functioning of Social Systems as a Defence Against Anxiety*. Tavistock Pamphlet No.3. London: Tavistock Institute of Human Relations.

Minty, B. and Patterson, G. (1994) 'The nature of child neglect.' *British Journal of Social Work 24*, 734–747.

NCB (1983) *Who Cares? – Young People in Care Speak Out*. London: NCB.

NCH (1996) *Factfile 96/97*. London: NCH.

Newell, P. (1991) *The UN Convention and Children's Rights in the UK*. London: NCB.

Oakley, A. (1982) *Subject Women*. London: Fontana.

Oliver, T. (1979) 'West Indian childhood.' In M. Hoyles (ed) *Changing Childhood.* London: Writers and Readers Publishing Co-operative.

OPCS (1989) *Surveys of Disability in the UK.* London: HMSO.

Parker, R. and Milham, S. (1989) 'Introduction: research on organisation and accountability for state intervention.' In J. Hudson and B. Galaway (eds) *The State as Parent.* NATO ASI series D, Vol. 53.

Parker, R., Ward, H., Jackson, S., Aldgate, J. and Wedge, P. (1991) *Assessing Outcomes in Child Care.* London: HMSO.

Parton, N. (1991) *Governing the Family: Child Care, Child Protection and the State.* Basingstoke: Macmillan.

Phillipson, J. (1992) *Practicing Equality – Women, Men and Social Work.* London: CCETSW.

Pizzey, S. and Davis, J. (1995) *A Guide for Guardians ad Litem in Public Law Proceedings under the Children Act 1989.* London: HMSO.

Plotnikoff, J. and Woolfson, R. (1996) *Reporting to Court under the Children Act.* London: HMSO.

Pugh, G. and De'Ath, E. (1984) *The Needs of Parents.* London: Macmillan.

Pugh, G., De'Ath, E. and Smith, C. (1994) *Confident Parents, Confident Children: Policy and Practice in Parent Education and Support.* London: NCB.

Reder, P., Duncan, S. and Gray, M. (1993) *Beyond Blame – Child Abuse Tragedies Revisited.* London: Routledge.

Rogers, C.M. and Wrightsman, L.S. (1978) 'Attitudes towards children's rights: nurturance or self determination.' *Journal of Social Issues 34,* 2.

Rogers, W.S., Hevey, D. and Ash, E. (1989) (eds) *Child Abuse and Neglect – Facing the Challenge.* Milton Keynes: OUP.

Rowe, J., Hundleby, M. and Garnett, L. (1989) 'Child care now.' *Research Series No.6.* London: BAAF.

Royal Society (1992) *Risk Analysis, Perception and Management: Report of a Royal Society Study Group.* London: The Royal Society.

Sgroi, S.A. (1982) *Handbook of Clinical Intervention in Child Sexual Abuse.* Lexington: Lexington Books.

Shaw, M. (1989) *Social Work and Children's Rights.* Paper presented at a conference at the University of Leicester School of Medical Sciences 19 April 1989.

Sheldon, B. (1980) *The Use of Contracts in Social Work.* Practice Notes Series, No.1. Birmingham: BASW.

Siporin, M. (1975) *Introduction to Social Work Practice.* New York and London: Collier Macmillan.

Smith, D. (1965) 'Front line organisation of the state mental hospital.' *Administrative Science Quarterly 10,* 381–99.

Stevenson, O. (1989) (ed) *Child Abuse: Professional Practice and Public Policy.* London: Harvester Wheatsheaf.

Stone, M. (1992) *Child Protection: A Model for Risk Assessment in Physical Abuse/Neglect.* Thames Ditton: Surrey County Council.

Stoppard, M. (1983) *The Baby Care Book.* London: Dorling Kindersley.

Timms, N. and Timms, R. (1982) *Dictionary of Social Welfare.* London: RKP.

UNICEF (1991) *The State of the World's Children.* Oxford: OUP.

Utting, W. (1991) *Children in the Public Care – A Review of Residential Care.* London: SSI/HMSO.

Van Every, J. (1992) 'Who is the family? The assumptions of British social policy.' *Critical Social Policy 33,* 62–75.

Wagner Report (1988) *Residential Care: A Positive Choice.* London: NISW.

White, R. (1983) 'Written agreements with families.' *Adoption and Fostering 7,* 4, 24–28.

Wise, S. (1985) *Becoming a Feminist Social Worker.* Manchester: Department of Sociology, University of Manchester.

Wise, S. (1988) *Doing Feminist Social Work.* Manchester: Department of Sociology, University of Manchester.

WO (1991) *Accommodating Children: A Review of Children's Homes in Wales.* Cardiff: WO.

Further Reading

Corby, B. (1993) *Child Abuse – Towards a Knowledge Base.* Buckingham: OUP.

EOC (1987) *Women and Men in Britain – A Research Profile.* London: HMSO.

Merrick, D. (1996) *Social Work and Abuse.* London: Routledge.

Owen, H. and Pritchard, J. (1993) *Good Practice in Child Protection.* London: Jessica Kingsley Publishers.

Walton, R. (1980) (ed) *Residential Care – A Reader in Current Theory and Practice.* London: Pergammon.

Subject Index

Author Index